Arguing A.I.

SAM WILLIAMS

ARGUING A.I.

The Battle for Twenty-first-Century Science

ATRANDOM.COM

NEW YORK

ATRANDOM.COM BOOKS and colophon are registered trademarks
of Random House, Inc.

Library of Congress Cataloging-in-Publication Data

Williams, Sam.
Arguing A.I.: the battle for twenty-first-century science/[Sam Williams].
p. cm.
Includes bibliographical references.
ISBN 0-8129-9180-X (pbk.)
1. Artificial intelligence. I. Title.

Q335 .W55 2001
006.3—dc21   2001053292

Website address: www.atrandom.com

2 4 6 8 9 7 5 3

First Edition

TO STEVE WILLIAMS, FIRST READER

AND FIRST SUPPORTER

Acknowledgments

Thanks to Aaron Oas for coming up with the initial idea that led to this book. Thanks to Henning Gutmann for assisting in the early development of that idea and to Mary Bahr at AtRandom.com Books for embracing it. Thanks also to SIBL, the New York Public Library's Science, Industry, and Business Library, a truly great resource in a truly great city.

Special thanks to Sunshine Lucas for her editorial patience and constructive criticism, to Bonnie Thompson and Beth Pearson for ironing out the wrinkles in my prose, and to Kate Blum for all her help with publicity.

Finally, special thanks and love to my wife, Tracy, not only for nurturing this book during its embryonic stages but also for putting up with the late nights and lost weekends that went into making it a reality.

Contents

Introduction

As the title suggests, this book is less about artificial intelligence—i.e., the science of building machines that mimic or augment human intelligence—than about the debate surrounding it.

Since its emergence in the years immediately following World War II, the field of artificial intelligence has been home to one of the fiercest intellectual battles in modern science. Like the debate over evolution a century ago, it is a battle in which faith and ego play as much a role as fact.

The comparison with evolution is double-edged. In many ways, the debate over artificial intelligence is undergoing its own subtle evolution. The last five years have triggered a changing of the guard in terms of the debate's leading participants. What was once a discussion largely confined to academic circles has opened up into a mainstream debate as a growing number of engineers and lay authors weigh in on the acceleration of modern technology and the future of mankind. Given the rapid emergence of the Internet, continuous exponential increases in computing power, and recent, notable breakthroughs such as Deep Blue's 1997 victory over human chess champion Garry Kasparov, writers are no longer asking "how" or "if" artificial intelligence will reach the level of human intelligence so much as "when?"

Indiana University professor Douglas Hofstadter, author of the 1979 Pulitzer Prize–winning A.I. treatise *Gödel, Escher, Bach,* summed up the recent trend in a speech to colleagues in July 2000:

"More or less simultaneously in the closing year of the twentieth century, there came out a curious coterie of books whose central, sensational-sounding claim was that humanity was on the verge of producing its own successors." Hofstadter cited as examples of this trend Raymond Kurzweil's *The Age of Spiritual Machines,* Hans Moravec's *Robot: Mere Machine to Transcendent Mind,* and Bill Joy's much-publicized *Wired* magazine essay "Why the Future Doesn't Need Us," works and authors that will appear in the coming chapters.

For Hofstadter, a scientist famous for defending the possibility of machine consciousness, the current trend is a troubling one. Although writers such as Kurzweil, Moravec, and Joy seem to defend the notion of sentient machines appearing in the near future, they do so with an almost casual disregard for the monumental difficulties of A.I. research. The evolution of machine intelligence, like the evolution of human intelligence, is a self-driven, self-optimizing process, these new authors argue. As machines become faster and more powerful, the ability to improve the design of the next generational cycle becomes that much easier. Witness the speedy ascendance of programs such as Deep Blue.

"The irony of this vision is its profound anti-intellectualism," notes Hofstadter. Should such a vision come to pass, it would mean a future in which machines know all there is to know about humans and human intelligence, with humans knowing little or nothing about machine intelligence in return. "We will indeed have built thinking beings," Hofstadter supposes, "and yet we will not have designed them ourselves, nor will we have the foggiest idea what their operating principles are."

In the forty-five years since the term "artificial intelligence" first appeared in scientific journals, the field of artificial intelligence has been no stranger to controversy. Deep Blue notwithstanding, many leading A.I. researchers see the community's continued inability to come up with a central theory of intelligence or a central theory of consciousness as evidence of an underlying structural failure. Some even go so far as to compare the entire A.I. field with the medieval protoscience of alchemy. No matter how many theories scientists throw up at the wall, nothing seems to stick. Why is this? The generous answer is to note the exceedingly complex nature of the subjects under scrutiny—that is, human intelligence and the human mind. Unlike their counterparts in the chemistry lab or the physics department, A.I. researchers have found their efforts to break intelligence down into a few foundational precepts continually rebuffed. Together with meteorologists, economists, and evolutionary theorists, they have spent much of the post–World War II period honing the mathematical models and scientific tools necessary for the study of chaotic, complex systems. Only now, after a half century's worth of effort, are the pieces of the puzzle even becoming discernible.

The harsh answer is to point out the artificial-intelligence research community's well-established reputation for scientific hubris. The fact that today's researchers see intelligence as a complex quagmire doesn't erase the fact that many of the field's earliest proponents saw intelligence in much simpler terms. To early pioneers such as Alan Turing, John McCarthy, and Allen Newell, artificial intelligence was the scientific world's equivalent of a limited land war. The brain was small, and machines were big. As long as the field continued to attract the best and the brightest, victory was never in question. The only disagreements seemed to be over how long that victory would take: five years or ten?

Given such early misconceptions, it's not hard to understand why the debate over artificial intelligence has remained so hot for so long. Still, if the words of Kurzweil et al. are to attract any supporters, one would expect them to come from within the traditional A.I. research community. As Hofstadter's words indicate, the support has been lukewarm at best. The natural response is to ask, "Why?"

Citing Deep Blue and Moore's Law, Kurzweil and his cohorts see the emergence of machines exhibiting human-level intelligence as a form of technological manifest destiny.[1] Once the average computer system reaches the computational power and structural complexity of the human brain—an event that, if measured in raw hardware terms, should occur between the years 2020 and 2030—the emergence of fully intelligent machines will become an almost foregone conclusion.

"Evolution's greatest creation—human intelligence—is providing the means for the next stage of evolution, which is technology," writes Kurzweil in *The Age of Spiritual Machines*. "This next stage of evolution was necessarily created by human intelligence itself, another example of the exponential engine of evolution using its innovations from one period (human beings) to create the next (intelligent machines)."[2]

Whether Deep Blue turns out be the Lucy or the Piltdown Man of artificial intelligence remains to be seen, but this tension over the future of technology merits study. Coming on the heels of the last decade's Y2K hysteria, it reflects the growing suspicion, even within engineering circles, that technology has already slipped the bonds of human control. It also reflects the growing divide between those who see intelligence in anthropocentric terms and those who do not. The tension essentially boils down to a modern update of the old Zen koan: If a machine does something smart but no human is there to design it or benefit from it, does the machine qualify as intelligent? Like most Zen koans, the answer is neither obvious nor helpful. What is helpful is the insight gained by examining the strengths and weaknesses of each viewpoint.

The specter of Darwin haunts both sides of the renewed A.I. debate. From the Kurzweil perspective, mechanical evolution is merely the continuation of human evolution "by other means." From the perspective of Kurzweil's critics, most notably Jaron Lanier, author of the 2000 *Wired* article "One-Half of a Manifesto: Why Stupid Software Will Save the Future from Neo-Darwinian Machines," evolution is a helpful metaphor for studying the technological world but only that, a metaphor. Although both sides may disagree on how much faith to put in Darwin, they seem to agree on the basic terms of engagement: Computer systems have gotten faster, smarter, and more organic over the last decade, making comparisons with biological systems less far-fetched than they once were.

A.I. isn't the only field experiencing a recent spate of evolutionary revisionism. Since the 1975 publication of Richard Dawkins's neo-Darwinian classic *The Selfish Gene,* authors have imported evolutionary theory into fields as wide-ranging as human psychology (David Buss's *The Evolution of Desire*), political science (Richard Wright's *Nonzero*), and human history (Jared Diamond's *Guns, Germs, and Steel*).

Such revisionism reflects what Tufts University philosopher Daniel Dennett, author of the 1998 book *Darwin's Dangerous Idea,* calls the "universal acid" nature of Darwinian theory.[3] Like a solvent that eats away everything, including its own container, Darwin's "dangerous idea" that natural selection, variation, and competition are enough to explain the evolution of most complex systems is quietly burning its way through modern culture. Once it passes through everything, Dennett assures us, we are "left with stronger, sounder versions of our most important ideas."

Granted, Dennett has his own ulterior motives for advancing this process. As a steadfast opponent of Cartesian dualism, the school of philosophy that sees the body and mind as distinct entities, Dennett has spent the last three decades battling fellow scholars' attempts to depict the mind as anything more than the complex, collective output of an underlying biochemical machine, read: the brain. His 1991 book *Consciousness Explained* has provided an intellectual platform for bullish A.I. authors such as Kurzweil and Moravec.

In *Darwin's Dangerous Idea,* however, Dennett provides colorful insight as to why Kurzweil, Moravec, and others would begin the twenty-first century by looking back to one of the leading minds of the nineteenth century for inspiration. Like the debate over evolution, the debate over artificial intelligence has absorbed new participants and new perspectives over time. Unlike the former debate, however, the debate over A.I. has done so without building upon a set of fundamental underlying principles. Nearly a century and a half after Darwin wrote *The Origin of Species,* scientists still debate various aspects of Darwinian theory, but the central theory of evolution via natural selection remains, in Dennett's words, "like Gulliver tied down in Lilliput."[4] Each new piece of evidence, whether it be Gregor Mendel's pea plants, Watson and Crick's DNA double helix, or the latest breakthroughs in genetic engineering, reinforces the stability of the overall system. In the battle for scientific survival, Darwin has grown stronger with each passing year.

The current outpouring of A.I.-related books, papers, manifestos, and "half manifestos" suggests an attempt to pin down that field in similar fashion. Frustrated by the research community's perceived lack of progress, authors have turned to Darwinian theory in an attempt to skirt the intellectual sand traps that have hampered the discipline for so long. Thanks to Darwin, what was once a battle between philosophers and scientists has become a battle between engineers and software developers. While not everybody accepts the new terms of this debate, its metamorphosis parallels the evolution of high technology over the last half-century. Like the computer, the A.I. debate has become more accessible, more dumbed-down with time. It has also become more beholden to complex forces, including market dynamics and public mood.

Simply put, the current tension over artificial intelligence is a reflection of our own society's tension over the future and what it holds. Authors are using the natural milestone provided by a fresh century to look back on the achievements and mistakes of the last. This tactic is nothing new. In fact, as we shall soon see, it is the tactic that gave birth to the science of artificial intelligence in the first place. Still, it is something we should keep in mind as we listen to both sides of the A.I. debate.

A.I. Debate Timeline

1900 David Hilbert's "Mathematical Problems" speech lays the foundation for twentieth-century mathematics and ignites many of the intellectual arguments that will give birth to both computer science and artificial intelligence.

1910 Publication of *Principia Mathematica,* Bertrand Russell and Alfred North Whitehead's attempt to provide a more philosophically sound foundation for modern mathematics.

1920 Einstein's general theory of relativity extends the post–Euclidean geometry work of Hilbert and other nineteenth-century mathematicians into the realm of physics. In the process, Einstein demonstrates that the viewpoint and motion of the observer are as important as the event being observed when factoring cosmological phenomena.

1921 Publication of *Tractatus Logico-philosophicus,* by Ludwig Wittgenstein, applying the Russell-Whitehead approach to language itself. All metaphysical debates stem from the inconsistencies and loopholes of human language, Wittgenstein argues, and such debates will become unnecessary once the hidden, logical structure of language is determined.

1927 Werner Heisenberg proposes that "uncertainty" is a fixed constant when examining the behavior of subatomic particles. In other words, an observer can never be entirely certain of a particle's position or direction, because the act of observation automatically affects the system being observed. Like relativity, Heisenberg's uncertainty principle becomes a weapon for philosophers who dismiss all forms of objective scientific inquiry as subjective inquiry in disguise.

1931 Kurt Gödel's "incompleteness theorem" provides the death-blow to the thirty-year Hilbert "program." Gödel proves the incompleteness of arithmetic as a logic-based system and, by extension, the susceptibility of any complex formal system to logical inconsistencies. Later A.I. critics will use this as proof that human intelligence, with its ability to identify and overcome logical paradoxes, cannot be replicated through formal logic or mechanical processes.

1936 Alan Turing's paper "On Computable Numbers" extends Gödel's arguments while offering a machine's-eye view of formal logic. Introducing a theoretical device called the "logical computing machine," Turing lays out a mechanical method for executing any arithmetically defined function, or algorithm. Turing thereby introduces a new field of mathematics dubbed computation.

1938 "A Symbolic Analysis of Relay and Switching Circuits," a master's thesis paper by MIT graduate student Claude Shannon, applies nineteenth-century forms of symbolic logic developed by Gottlob Frege and George Boole to the science of electromechanical relays and telephone networks. This paper lays out the foundation for information theory and future investigations of human cognition from an electromechanical perspective.

1939 World War II begins in Europe. Turing goes to work for the British government as a code-breaking expert, employing many of the ideas laid out in "On Computable Numbers."

1940 Turing and his Bletchley Park colleagues develop a series of devices, dubbed "bombes," capable of calculating the massive numbers needed to decode encrypted radio messages.

1943 "A Logical Calculus of the Ideas Immanent in Nervous Activity," by Warren McCullough and Walter Pitts, introduces the neuron model of the brain. The authors liken the brain to a large telephone network composed of binary state (i.e., on or off) neuronal "switches."

1944 Stanford professor and former Hilbert student George Polya publishes *How to Solve It,* a book that attempts to lay out a mathematical approach to problem solving. Polya dubs this new field of mathematics "heuristics."

1944 Turing and fellow Bletchley Park researchers complete construction of Colossus, an 1,800-vacuum-tube device used to break down encoded German messages.

1945 U.S. engineers John W. Mauchly, John P. Eckert, et al. complete the construction of ENIAC, a machine considered by most technology historians to be the first modern computer.

1947 University of Illinois researcher Arthur Samuel begins his first experiments with computer checkers.

1948 *Cybernetics, or Control and Communication in the Animal and the Machine,* by MIT professor Norbert Wiener, argues that the human nervous system and mechanical communications systems such as the Bell Telephone network are indistinguishable, at least from a theoretical perspective.

1948   The Hixon Symposium on Cerebral Mechanisms and Behavior at Caltech hosts the first major gathering by psychologists, mathematicians, and electrical engineers to discuss the electromechanical nature of the human brain. "The General and Logical Theory of Automata," a lecture by Hungarian mathematician John von Neumann, introduces the notion that all life can be boiled down to self-reproducing systems following fixed mathematical rules.

1950   "Computing Machinery and Intelligence," by Alan Turing, introduces the Imitation Game—later dubbed the Turing test. If a machine can make a human believe he is communicating with another human, argues Turing, the machine must be considered intelligent.

1950   EDVAC, a successor to ENIAC, becomes operational. The first computer to employ internally stored programs, EDVAC is also the first to incorporate the full universal computing principles laid out in Turing's 1936 paper.

1950   Claude Shannon, the father of information theory, writes his first recognized paper on computer chess, "Programming a Digital Computer for Playing Chess."

1956   The Dartmouth Summer Conference on Artificial Intelligence initiates the first official use of the term "artificial intelligence."

1956   Allen Newell and Herbert Simon introduce Logic Theorist, a program based on the heuristic principles of George Polya. The forerunner of modern expert systems, Logic Theorist has the ability to prove mathematical theorems through the logical application of fixed axioms. Later researchers and philosophers dub this approach to A.I. "symbolic manipulation."

1957 Allen Newell and Herbert Simon unveil the General Problem Solver, a more robust follow-up to Logic Theorist. GPS solves puzzles and word problems through a cybernetic feedback technique dubbed "means-ends analysis."

1957 *Syntactic Structures,* by Noam Chomsky, approaches the study of linguistics from a computer-science perspective. Chomsky posits that language can be studied according to its own internal logic and rules, launching the "Chomskian revolution" in linguistics. Chomsky's investigations would eventually determine that biological factors play a key role in language comprehension, however, contradicting and undermining the artificial-intelligence community's attempts to build natural language systems *ex situ.*

1958 John McCarthy develops the LISP programming language, a major foundational tool for A.I. programming.

1958 With "Heuristic Problem Solving: The Next Advance in Operations Research," Carnegie Institute professors Herbert A. Simon and Allen Newell publish their first paper on GPS and use it to predict dramatic breakthroughs in machine intelligence over the coming decade, including the first computer chess champion.

1958 John McCarthy and Marvin Minsky found the Artificial Intelligence Laboratory at MIT.

1960 "Mind, Machines and Gödel," by J. R. Lucas, argues that Gödel's incompleteness theorem sets a trap that no machine can cross. The mind is therefore not a machine, says Lucas, because it can overcome or sidestep the paradoxes that snare machines beholden to formal logic.

1962 Arthur Samuel's computer checkers program defeats Robert W. Nealey, a former state checkers champion of Connecticut.

1963 John McCarthy leaves MIT and moves to Stanford, where he founds the Stanford Artificial Intelligence Laboratory.

1965 Hubert Dreyfus writes "Alchemy and Artificial Intelligence" as a memo for Rand Corp. He calls the lack of progress in computer chess since Newell and Simon's 1957 prediction a sign of A.I. researchers' overoptimism and cites the recent example of a computer chess program being defeated by a "ten-year-old novice" as evidence of stagnation in the field.

1965 With "ELIZA: A Computer Program for the Study of Natural Language Communication Between Man and Machine," MIT scientist Joseph Weizenbaum introduces ELIZA, a program designed to mimic the behavior of a Rogerian psychotherapist.

1967 MacHack, a computer program written by MIT A.I. lab hacker Richard Greenblatt, defeats A.I. critic Hubert Dreyfus after the author is challenged to a public chess match.

1969 *Perceptrons,* by Marvin Minsky and Seymour Papert, exposes the theoretical weaknesses in perceptron, or "neural net," theory. Although Minsky had been a past champion of neural-net research, the book is generally credited for stifling funding for neural-net research until the mid-1980s. It also reflects the increasingly competitive nature of A.I. research in the late 1960s.

1972 *What Computers Can't Do,* by Hubert Dreyfus, expands upon his earlier "Alchemy and Artificial Intelligence." Dreyfus paints the science of A.I. as the culmination of the Western philosophical tradition, which seeks to compartmentalize the universe through logic and rigid categorization. As such, A.I. is more a philosophical viewpoint than a science, Dreyfus argues.

1976 MYCIN, an expert system designed to diagnose infectious blood diseases, is introduced by cocreators Edward Shortliffe and Bruce Buchanan.

1976 *Computer Power and Human Reason,* by MIT professor Joseph Weizenbaum, brands most contemporary A.I. research as "tinkering" and distanced from the needs of modern society. Weizenbaum also questions the overall ethics of the field. "Since we do not now have ways of making computers wise, we ought not to give computers tasks that demand wisdom."

1979 *Gödel, Escher, Bach,* by Douglas Hofstadter, bludgeons into submission the Gödel debate initiated by Lucas in 1960. It points to numerous instances in which the Gödelian incompleteness of formal systems actually provides primitive evidence of system self-awareness.

1980 "Mind, Brains and Programs," by John. R. Searle, offers the first appearance of the "Chinese room" argument against machine sentience and challenges Hofstadter's "strong A.I." interpretation of intelligence.

1983 Texas researcher Doug Lenat launches the Cyc project. It is the largest-scale effort to date to create a knowledge base broad enough to replicate the commonsense rules all humans use in day-to-day reasoning.

1985 Symbolics, one of the first companies to offer commercial artificial-intelligence software, posts $100 million in annual sales.

1985 *Society of Mind,* by Marvin Minsky, culminates the A.I. research community's two-decade migration away from interpreting the mind as a symbol-manipulating machine. Minsky instead presents the mind as a messy kludge of parallel, and occasionally overlapping, processes.

1988 *Mind Children: The Future of Robot and Human Intelligence,* by Hans Moravec, advances the notion that, if current technology trends continue, intelligent robots will replace humans sometime during the first half of the twenty-first century.

1990 *The Age of Intelligent Machines,* by Ray Kurzweil, predicts, among other things, the first defeat of a human champion by a computer chess program in 1998.

1990 *The Emperor's New Mind,* by Roger Penrose, raises the notion that quantum physics might allow for the brain's ability to evade the logical loopholes that snare most machines.

1991 *Consciousness Explained,* by Daniel Dennett, argues that consciousness, the phenomenon Searle and other contemporary philosophers hold up as the last distinguishing feature separating human thought from mechanical computation, is in fact an ambient effect of biomechanical processes. "Conscious human minds are more-or-less serial virtual machines implemented—inefficiently—on the parallel hardware that evolution has provided for us," writes Dennett.

1993 Symbolics, whose annual sales have fallen to $10 million from $100 million eight years before, files for Chapter 11 protection.

1997 Deep Blue, an IBM supercomputer running a software chess program, defeats world chess champion Garry Kasparov in a six-match series. Afterward, Dennett and Dreyfus square off in a televised debate over the significance of the victory on *NewsHour with Jim Lehrer.*

1999 *The Age of Spiritual Machines,* by Ray Kurzweil, expands upon the author's previous A.I. predictions. Kurzweil calls machine evolution an extension of biological evolution and predicts that machines and humans will be mutually indistinguishable by the end of the twenty-first century.

2000 "Why the Future Doesn't Need Us," a *Wired* magazine cover story by UNIX architect Bill Joy, echoes Weizenbaum's concern about the ethics of modern science and artificial intelligence. Although Joy accepts Kurzweil's view that technology is evolving free of centralized human control, he views this evolution as dangerous to humanity.

2000 "One-Half of a Manifesto," by Jaron Lanier, challenges both the nightmare visions of Joy and the techno-rapture of Moravec and Kurzweil. Yes, Lanier says, machines are getting more powerful, but the human minds responsible for tapping that power have yet to overcome the obstacles to scalable software design. Lanier echoes Dreyfus's claim that A.I. is more a faith system than a science.

Arguing A.I.

Chapter 1

—

THE INSPIRATION:

HILBERT AND TURING

At the height of the Second International Congress of Mathematicians in Paris in August 1900, German mathematician David Hilbert offered a poetic introduction to what would later be known as his "Twenty-three Problems" lecture, a milestone speech many mathematical historians credit for laying the foundation of twentieth-century mathematics [http://aleph0.clarku.edu/~djoyce/hilbert/problems.html]. "Who among us would not be glad to lift the veil behind which the future lies hidden, to cast a glance at the next advances of our science and the secrets of its development in future centuries?" he asked.

A hundred years later, Hilbert's words offer a poetic introduction to the history of artificial intelligence as well. Artificial intelligence is, after all, a science inextricably linked to the future. Read any book on A.I. and it's easy to detect a similar desire to bear witness to the future. The desire to "lift the veil" separating today's earnest investigation from tomorrow's common knowledge is as strong for A.I. researchers as it was for Hilbert and his colleagues a century ago.

The similarity is a familial one. Although the science of artificial intelligence as we now know it didn't emerge until a full decade after Hilbert's death in 1943, many of the theories that gave rise to that science descend directly from ideas posed by Hilbert at that fateful Paris lecture. The same goes for the spirit of artificial intelligence. Conceived in the collaborative science projects of World War II and nurtured in the postwar era of big science, A.I., too, draws its heritage from the post-Paris "program" created by Hilbert and his disciples at Germany's Göttingen University in the decades prior to the Nazi seizure of power.

"Hilbert was a giant among mathematicians," writes mathematical historian Mary Tiles in *Mathematics and the Image of Reason.* "It is hard to overestimate his influence over the character of twentieth century mathematics; so many of the great names in mathematics worked under him or worked with him."

Hilbert was born in 1862 and raised in the East Prussian city of Königsberg. Now the Russian city of Kaliningrad, Königsberg in the nineteenth century was best known as the home of the eighteenth-century Prussian philosopher Immanuel Kant. Growing up in Kant's prodigious intellectual wake, Hilbert developed an early affinity for numbers and logic that would prompt him to pursue a career in mathematics, much to the consternation of his father, Otto Hilbert, a Prussian judge.

Like Kant, Hilbert saw mathematics as the vehicle through which the human mind displayed its ultimate capacity for reason. Both men echoed the sentiments of Plato, who, according to legend, had the statement "Let no man ignorant of geometry enter here" inscribed over the doorway of his Athenian Academy as a testament to the relationship between mathematics and critical thinking.

Kant argued that the mathematical discipline of geometry offered evidence of the mind's innate, or a priori, reasoning abilities. Science, Kant said, bases its discoveries on empirical observation, but geometry, which rests atop the abstract postulates first outlined in Euclid's *Elements,* generates notions of space and time that anticipate empirical observation. According to Kant, this anticipation was more than just a coincidence. It was an indicator of the human mind's ability to give shape to the universe even before it was observed.

"There can be no doubt that all our knowledge begins with experience," wrote Kant in the introduction to his masterwork, *Critique of Pure Reason* [www.arts.cuhk.edu.hk/Philosophy/Kant/cpr/]. "But though all our knowledge begins with experience it does not follow that it all arises out of experience." Such ideas flew in the face of the empiricist school of philosophy, a branch led by British intellectuals such as David Hume, George Berkeley, and John Locke. Together, these men saw the mind as little more than a blank slate, a device much like a loom or a refractive lens that requires tangible input in order to generate meaningful output. "All our ideas or more feeble perceptions are copies of our impressions," wrote Hume in his 1758 book *Enquiry Concerning Human Understanding* [www.utm.edu/ research/hume/wri/lenq/lenq.htm], adding later that "the unexperienced reasoner is no reasoner at all."

Kant's eighteenth-century views took a beating throughout the nineteenth century as mathematicians earnestly probed the structural weaknesses of Euclidean geometry. While studying at the University of Königsberg, Hilbert delivered a defense of Kant's "synthetic" a priori arguments in the realm of arithmetical judgment,[1] and in 1899 he published *Grundlangen der Geometrie* (*Foundations of Geometry*), a virtuoso work that fused the mathematics of Euclidean and non-Euclidean geometry into a single, theoretically sound structure. As a personal tribute to his countryman, Hilbert used a Kant quotation for the book's epigraph: "All human knowledge begins with intuitions, then passes to concepts and ends with ideas."

In the course of defending Kant, Hilbert experienced a profound epiphany: Arguments over Euclidean postulates were really just arguments over symbolic relationships. Infinite planes, parallel lines, and right angles were little more than window dressing, elegant, man-made devices designed to make the underlying concepts more appealing to the human eye. "One must be able to say at all times— instead of points, straight lines, and planes—tables, chairs, and beer mugs," quipped Hilbert to an academic colleague, summing up his abstract approach to both geometry and mathematics as a whole.

By the time of his Paris speech, Hilbert, then thirty-eight, had built up a sizable reputation as a mathematical reformer. Following *Foundations,* he was soon looking for new challenges. His intuition told him that the rest of mathematics, particularly arithmetic, geometry's logical cousin, was ripe for a similar overhaul. If mathematicians could prove it to be both *consistent* and *complete*—that is, none of its foundational axioms contradicted one another or left room for loopholes—Kant and Plato's vision of mathematics as man's innate link to the infinite might be that much closer to proof.

Sensing that such a project was beyond the capacity of a single mathematician, Hilbert set out to make it a collaborative crusade. He spent the spring and most of the summer of 1900 preparing a speech for the Paris Congress that would rally other mathematicians to the reformist cause.

During that speech, Hilbert gave voice to his philosophical vision. Citing what he called the "axiom of provability," Hilbert insisted that all mathematicians work with the conviction that problems exist to be solved. As a devoté of truth, Hilbert objected to the so-called revolt from reason led by nineteenth-century philosophers such as Friedrich Nietzsche and even scientists such as Sigmund Freud. In Hilbert's view, mathematics represented the last bastion of rational thought in a world increasingly given over to irrationality, instinct, and subjective interpretation. To drive this conflict home, Hilbert alluded to the old Latin proverb *Ignoramus et ignorabimus* ("Ignorant we are, and ignorant we shall remain") during his speech. It was a phrase that had enjoyed popularity among nineteenth-century Romantic thinkers, and Hilbert wished to hold it up for public ridicule. "In mathematics there is no *ignorabimus,*" he told his colleagues. "We hear within us the perpetual call: There is the problem. Seek its solution. You can find it by pure reason."

Following the philosophical introduction, Hilbert laid out ten of the twenty-three major problems he considered most important to the future development of mathematics. Some of the problems were specific: a solution to Fermat's last theorem. Some were general: the restructuring of physics according to mathematical axioms, for example. By the speech's end, the assembled audience was more interested in arguing about the specific details of each problem than discussing the overarching anti-*ignorabimus* philosophy espoused by Hilbert.

Within a decade, however, Hilbert's twenty-three problems had become an agenda of sorts. As the head of the Göttingen mathematics department, Hilbert used his power to build what became known as the "Göttingen program," a collective effort to tackle the twenty-three problems on the Paris list. Chief among them was Problem No. 2, dubbed the *Entscheidungsproblem* by Hilbert's German students, an attempt to prove the completeness and consistency of arithmetic.

Just as the encyclopedic tendencies of Enlightenment thinkers would trigger the Romantic backlash in the nineteenth century, so too would the philosophies of Hilbert and his peers trigger a similar backlash in the twentieth. The backlash came in the form of three proofs, all of which would have a major impact on the future science of artificial intelligence. In 1932, Czech mathematician Kurt Gödel published a paper that counteracted the Hilbert quest for a proof of arithmetic completeness. Any formal system large enough to include the logic of arithmetic, Gödel argued, was large enough to include "true" statements unprovable under the logical rules of that formal system.

Although the language was esoteric, the logic was inescapable. No matter how many axioms Hilbert and his students produced, there would always be room for logical loopholes, statements that said, in effect, "This statement is unprovable in this formal system." To make this logic even more maddening to Hilbert and his colleagues, Gödel expressed his argument numerically, relying on the power of infinity to provide abundant room for the "Gödel numbers" that existed outside any finite mathematical system. In one fell swoop, Gödel had reinserted the verb *ignorabimus* into the vocabulary of modern mathematics.

If this one blow wasn't enough, a two-blow combination in 1936 would finally do in the vaunted Hilbert program. That year, British mathematician Alan Turing and American logician Alonzo Church published simultaneous papers undermining the mathematical notion of "decidability," an outgrowth of the *Entscheidungsproblem*.[2] In order to prove completeness, Hilbert and his students first had to show that the mechanism of proof was itself free of holes. In investigating this side problem, Turing and Church found that there existed valid mathematical procedures, or algorithms, that could not be verified through mathematical logic.

Of the two papers, Turing's took the more creative approach. Instead of viewing the question as an issue of logic, Turing refashioned it as a matter of mechanical engineering. Machines are, by definition, mechanical. They execute invariable processes that are the embodiment of formal logic. In his 1936 paper "On Computable Numbers with an Application to the *Entscheidungsproblem*," Turing outlined the structure of an imaginary machine that did nothing but add and subtract numbers. Dubbing his device a "logical computing machine," Turing hypothesized that the device should be able to execute any finite arithmetic procedure by breaking it down into a series of logical steps [www.abelard.org/turpap2/turpap2.htm].

Although the design was imaginary—Turing pictured a tireless human clerk, or "computer," writing and erasing numbers one step at a time on an infinitely long tape—this "finite state" method has since become the elemental model for modern computation. Analyze the performance of any modern "computer"—a term once used to refer to humans, not machines—and you will find the same linear series of step-by-step logical procedures first envisioned by Turing. For this reason, today's computers are classified as "Turing machines."

For Turing, the logical computing machine was a colorful way to approach a multitude of major mathematical issues. Not only was this step-by-step process enough to perform any procedure requiring mathematical logic, it was enough to emulate the behavior of any mechanical system, period. Even with this skeleton-key capability, Turing, like Gödel before him, proved the existence of "true" statements that could not be generated by the machine alone, no matter how long the input tape, no matter how many computational steps it took. Once again, there was *ignorabimus* in mathematics, at least as far as the machine was concerned.

The publication of Turing's paper alongside Church's more complex paper effectively closed the book on Hilbert's Göttingen program. By 1936, the vaunted mathematics department had already fallen into decline. The Nazi Party's rise to power had led to the purging of Jewish faculty, decimating the department's staff and sending a demoralized Hilbert into retirement. Watching this decay from a distance, Hilbert refused to yield on his belief that mathematics was a discipline based on knowledge and proof, not incompleteness and uncertainty. Upon his death in 1943, the epitaph on his Göttingen tombstone sounded a final, optimistic note. Borrowing a line from one of his last speeches, it read, *"Wir mussen wissen. Wir werden wissen."* In English: "We must know. We will know."

———

Although few of Hilbert's former colleagues were still around to receive the message—many had emigrated to America and were lending their talents to the Allied war effort—the philosophy would find a new home in the scientific fields to emerge during the postwar period. Turing's paper, while closing the door on more than three decades' worth of work, opened up an entirely new door by introducing the science of computational theory.

Turing himself would be one of the first to recognize the expansive reaches of this new science. During the wartime years, the Cambridge scholar worked as a code-breaking specialist for the British government, helping design a few of the first primitive computing devices. Dubbed "bombes," these largely mechanical contraptions had no memory but still offered invaluable assistance in breaking down the large numbers associated with wartime decryption.

Across the Atlantic, American engineers and scientists were creating even more sophisticated devices. The first, dubbed ENIAC, short for Electronic Numerical Integrator and Computer, became operational just months after the war's completion. With eighteen thousand vacuum tubes and a weight of thirty tons, ENIAC boasted less memory capacity (sixteen kilobytes) than most of today's handheld video games.[3] Nevertheless, it was impressive enough to attract the attention of Hungarian mathematician and former Hilbert student John von Neumann. As mathematical adviser to the U.S. Army, von Neumann used his political influence to secure ENIAC's services in the ongoing Manhattan Project. In order to predict the outcome of several atomic-bomb tests, physicists at Los Alamos converted their calculations to punch-card form and shipped the cards off to the U.S. Army proving ground at Aberdeen, Maryland, ENIAC's home. The process was cumbersome, but the results came back in a fraction of the time it would have taken a team of human computers to calculate them. Von Neumann and his Los Alamos colleagues were duly impressed.

As a mathematician, von Neumann saw the link between ENIAC and the prewar paper put out by Turing. During the machine's design stage, he prodded military engineers John Mauchly and John Eckert to come up with a successor machine that would meet the theoretical specifications laid out by Turing in 1936. The result of this prodding was EDVAC, the first true Turing machine and the first computer boasting enough memory to tackle complex algorithmic procedures. Released in 1951, its design was foreshadowed by a von Neumann paper leaked to the academic community in 1945.[4]

Von Neumann's efforts paralleled similar work by Turing, who had kept abreast of postwar computing research via the Automatic Computing Engine, or ACE, a separate project in Great Britain. As early as 1944, Turing had discussed the prospects of "building a brain" mechanically. In 1947 Turing began examining ways to prove intelligent behavior in machines. That same year, he wrote a paper entitled "Intelligent Machinery," which examined the possible counterarguments against machine intelligence. Three years later, motivated by the critiques of philosophers already questioning the possibility of machine intelligence, Turing explored the topic even further, penning "Computing Machinery and Intelligence" for the philosophical journal *Mind* [www.abelard.org/turpap/turpap.htm].

Like Hilbert's Paris speech, Turing's paper opened with a provocative question: "Can machines think?" Fearing that the word "think" was too loaded, Turing proposed a way around the word via a qualitative test. Dubbed the "Imitation Game" by Turing, this test has since been renamed the Turing test in his honor.

To the modern reader, the instructions for Turing's Imitation Game read like a cross between the rules for a nineteenth-century parlor game and Jean-Paul Sartre's existentialist play *No Exit.* Turing specifies the need for three human participants. The first participant is an interrogator of either gender. The other two participants, one male, one female, are the respondents. The interrogator must sit in a separate room and can communicate with the respondents only via a Teletype. With no access to vocal or visual cues, the interrogator must determine the identity of the person on the other end of the line via the text coming through the Teletype. Turing further complicates this task by giving each respondent permission to mimic the typing and conversational style of the other. With these rules in place, the interrogator must now determine which respondent is the male and which respondent is the female through pointed questioning.

To make the game even more interesting, Turing proposes an added twist: What if, after a few minutes of back-and-forth dialogue, somebody replaces one of the respondents with a computer capable of playing the game just as well as a human? Blind to the switch, the only way for the interrogator to determine that a machine has entered the game is to judge the intelligence level of the responses. Supposing the replies are intelligent enough, is it conceivable that the interrogator might fail to detect the switch? Such a challenge would be heavily weighted against the machine, Turing notes, but a computer victory under these circumstances would be hard to dismiss.

"May not machines carry out something which ought to be described as thinking but which is very different from what man does?" wonders Turing, playing the momentary role of a skeptical observer. "This objection is a very strong one, but at least we can say that if, nevertheless, a machine can be constructed to play the imitation game successfully, we need not be troubled by the objection."[5]

The ultimate purpose of the Imitation Game, Turing writes, is to drive home the message that intelligence—like beauty—is in the eye of the beholder. Unless we are inside the machine seeing what it sees, thinking what it thinks, the only reliable test for intelligence is to measure its performance in situations that demand intelligent behavior.

"The original question, 'Can machines think?' I believe to be too meaningless to deserve discussion," Turing concludes. "Nevertheless, I believe at the end of the century the use of words and general educated opinion will have altered so much that one will be able to speak of machines thinking without expecting to be contradicted."

—

Fifty-one years after their publication, Turing's words seem prescient and naïve at the same time. Language and public opinion have certainly changed over the last half century. "User-friendly" computer interfaces and "personal" computers have reduced the emotional distance between human users and the monstrous machines of Turing's day. In a few very limited cases it is even safe to say that computers have crossed the Turing threshold. Garry Kasparov's comments [www.time.com/time/magazine/archive/1996/dom/960325/kasparov.html] in 1996 after watching Deep Blue employ a cunning pawn sacrifice move—"I could feel—I could smell—a new kind of intelligence across the table"—seem to reinforce Turing's closing assertions. For the most part, however, the notion of machines imitating humans in thought and behavior remains firmly fixed within the realm of science fiction. Few modern scientists equate savvy chess moves with general intelligence, just as few modern scientists equate the internal workings of a computer to the internal workings of a brain. At best, artificial-intelligence programs offer a tantalizing glimpse at the overall complexity of human intelligence; yet no matter how many times we "lift the veil" and expand that glimpse, another veil quickly appears.

Then again, the A.I. research community's willingness to soldier on, even without a clear long-term vision, remains its greatest attribute. Like Hilbert, a mathematician whose epitaph explicitly rejects the notion that some forms of knowledge should remain permanently hidden, A.I. researchers have learned to meet adversity with optimism. Today's A.I. researcher recognizes that for every closing door, a dozen new doors are opening up. The key to maintaining a robust discipline is guessing ahead of time which doors offer the most promising pathways beyond.

"History teaches the continuity of the development of science," said Hilbert to his colleagues in 1900. "We know that every age has its own problems, which the following age either solves or casts aside as profitless and replaces with new ones. If we would obtain an idea of the probable development of mathematical knowledge in the immediate future, we must let the unsettled questions pass before our minds and look over the problems which the science of today sets and whose solution we expect from the future. To such a review of problems the present day, lying at the meeting of the centuries, seems to me well adapted."

The centuries have changed but the words still resonate. As we shall soon see, the A.I. research community, its allies, and its opponents are collectively deciding which problems to "cast aside as profitless" and which problems still demand solving.

Chapter 2

—

THE PIONEER: JOHN MCCARTHY

To this day, John McCarthy can't quite recall when he first came across the term "artificial intelligence." As the chief organizer of the 1956 Dartmouth Summer Conference on Artificial Intelligence—the event that officially introduced "artificial intelligence" to the scientific community's vocabulary—McCarthy knows he didn't invent it on his own.

"I have this vague feeling of having heard it before," he says, "but I've never been able to figure out whether I did or didn't make it up. Who knows? I probably did make it up myself."

Given the fact that nobody else has stepped forward to claim credit, McCarthy is willing to go down in history as the man who coined the term. At age seventy-four, McCarthy remains deeply committed to the science and culture of artificial intelligence he helped create. A professor emeritus at Stanford, McCarthy has made his personal Web page a vital resource for students interested in the background and philosophy of A.I. It also offers a glimpse at the political philosophy that has shaped McCarthy's approach to science and technology [www.formal.stanford.edu/jmc].

"The earth is humanity's garden, and we should make it as productive as we can," writes McCarthy in one on-line essay [www.formal.stanford.edu/jmc/future/index.html]. "Within the limits of possibility, what humanity will do will be increasingly determined by what humanity wants to do."

Such views may seem conservative in today's political climate, but they draw on McCarthy's own Marxist, atheist background. Born in 1927 Boston, McCarthy grew up in a politically active family. His father, John Patrick McCarthy, worked as a longshoreman, carpenter, and occasional labor organizer on the docks. His mother, Ida, once led a student march on the White House in support of female suffrage in the decade before John's birth. Together, the two parents raised their children in a political context that saw science as a means toward improving the collective lot of the masses.

As a child, McCarthy showed a gift for mathematics. After his family headed west, McCarthy entered Caltech in 1944, where he studied for one year before getting thrown out for failing to attend mandatory physical-education classes. In Philip J. Hilts's 1982 book *Scientific Temperaments,* McCarthy recalled his subsequent induction into the U.S. Army, including the basic training that followed, as offering "relief" from the rigors of college. "They had a much worse obstacle course at Caltech," he says.[1]

After the war, McCarthy re-enrolled at Caltech. With no obstacle courses in his way, he promptly completed his undergraduate degree in 1948. Later that same year, McCarthy sat in on the Hixon Symposium, a conference on cerebral mechanisms held on the Caltech campus. There, McCarthy encountered von Neumann and other researchers who seemed flushed with excitement over the latest computer technologies just starting to emerge from wartime laboratories. "The Symposium had some really great psychologists," McCarthy says. "I didn't know how great they were until a few years later. They had [neuropsychology pioneer Karl] Lashley and [Wolfgang] Kohler, the scientist who had done all the experiments on ape intelligence in the 1920s."

Another prominent invitee was Manhattan Project mathematician John von Neumann. The Hixon Symposium offered von Neumann a forum to present his latest insights on the mathematics of self-reproducing systems. During the war, von Neumann's experiments with computation had only reinforced the mathematician's growing suspicion that all living processes can be boiled down to mathematically defined behavior. His paper for the symposium, entitled "The General and Logical Theory of Automata," took the Turing machine concept and applied it to the realm of biology, presenting the human genome as a computation system programmed to reproduce copies of itself. Written seven years before Watson and Crick's analysis of the DNA molecule, von Neumann's paper would anticipate the chemical mechanism for DNA transcription. It would also provide the basis for a future field of science: artificial life.

For McCarthy, von Neumann's lecture was simply one of many documenting the similarities between computation and lifelike behavior. The analogies were intriguing, but when it was all over, McCarthy sensed a blind spot in the dialogue. "Everybody was comparing computers with the brain, but nobody said anything about using computers to simulate intelligence," McCarthy recalls.

Following the symposium, McCarthy cooked up an experiment involving a computer program that modeled the relationship between a living organism and its surrounding environment. He sent it off to von Neumann, who, suitably impressed, suggested that McCarthy pursue his Ph.D studies at Princeton so that the two scientists could collaborate more easily. McCarthy took the advice, and though his proposed experiment never saw the light of day, he soon found himself embroiled in the budding fields of computer science, cybernetics, and automata studies.

While at Princeton, McCarthy fell in with a group of young researchers equally interested in using computers to simulate human intelligence. His first collaborator was Claude Shannon, a Bell Labs scientist and author of two landmark papers in the field of computer science. The first, a 1938 master's thesis titled "A Symbolic Analysis of Relay and Switching Circuits," revived the study of Boolean logic to explain how mechanical networks could be expressed as a series of binary on and off signals; the second, published in 1948, launched the science of information theory and coined the term "bit" as the basic unit of information in computer science. By 1950, Shannon had already turned his attention to computer programming, writing the first chess-playing software program.

While working in Shannon's lab, McCarthy encountered another future collaborator, a Harvard-educated mathematician named Marvin Minsky. Although the two men had been born the same year, Minsky's academic background offered an interesting counterpoint to McCarthy's. As a child, Minsky had moved from one prestigious school to the next, attending the Fieldstone School in Manhattan, the Bronx School of Science, and Phillips Academy before finally applying to Harvard. Prior to his admission to Harvard, Minsky, too, had spent the last year of the war in uniform, serving in the navy. After returning to Harvard, Minsky promptly developed a reputation as a scientific whiz kid, battling openly with psychology professors who refused to indulge his curiosity for neural networks—machine-based models for learning that took inspiration from the human brain's own neuronal structure.[2]

Together, Minsky, Shannon, and McCarthy formed the nucleus of a growing coterie of young scientists interested in charting the last untamed frontier of modern science: the human mind. The effort was much like the transcontinental railroad project of the late nineteenth century. From one end mathematicians and engineers were investigating the lifelike aspects of mechanical systems; from the other, biologists and psychologists were probing the mechanical composition of the brain. Both sides were making progress, but without a common agenda, they ran the risk of wasted effort and needless overlap.

In 1953 McCarthy decided to supply that agenda. Building mechanical brains was hard work, but so too was splitting the atom. If researchers attacked the problem en masse, as their Manhattan Project counterparts had done, their chances for success would be that much better. Soliciting the help of Shannon, McCarthy proposed a book that would offer a survey of papers from every corner of the new field. Before sending out the call for papers, however, Shannon and McCarthy needed a name for this as yet unnamed discipline.

"Shannon didn't want anything over the top, so we went with 'Automata Studies,'" recalls McCarthy. "The papers we got back were to some extent a disappointment to me. I was hoping for something more along the lines of what became artificial intelligence."[3]

Three years later, McCarthy had a chance to select a better name. By that point, both he and Minsky had moved on from Princeton, with McCarthy taking an adjunct professorship at Dartmouth and Minsky becoming a junior fellow at Harvard. McCarthy proposed a summer conference so that they and other like-minded researchers could compare notes and collaborate. At the time, McCarthy wanted to emulate some of the studies then being put together by the Defense Department. Rounding up Minsky, Shannon, and IBM scientist Nathaniel Rochester, McCarthy secured a grant from the Rockefeller Foundation and sent out a call for papers. This time, instead of "Automata Studies," he decided to go with a more thought-provoking title. The Dartmouth Summer Conference on Artificial Intelligence was born. "I wanted to nail the flag to the mast and make it clear to everybody what the goal was," says McCarthy, describing his first use of the term "artificial intelligence."

Not everybody bought into the term with the same level of enthusiasm. A group of Rand researchers who had been billing their work as "complex information processing" reluctantly decided to attend the conference despite concerns over its "floating crap game" appearance.[4] Led by Herbert Simon, a Carnegie Institute economist turned math professor, the group was putting the finishing touches on a program called Logic Theorist.

As a program, Logic Theorist was based on the mathematics of a Stanford professor named George Polya. In his 1945 book *How to Solve It,* Polya had outlined a form of mathematical decision-making called heuristics. Fusing formal logic and intelligent guessing, Polya demonstrated how a simple algorithmic procedure could filter a massive number of options—the number of chess moves available at the beginning of a game, for example—down to a few successful solutions. A decade later, Simon, along with fellow Rand researchers Allen Newell and Cliff Shaw, was finally putting Polya's maxims to work.

Although unfinished at the time of the conference, Logic Theorist easily led the pack when compared to the still-developing theories of Minsky and McCarthy. Such a head start inevitably created friction between egos as Simon and Newell quickly excused themselves to go back and finish the program. Still, when the scientists finally unveiled their work, the results were impressive. Simon and Newell fed Logic Theorist the basic theorems for fifty-two proofs taken from Bertrand Russell and Alfred North Whitehead's *Principia Mathematica.* The program came back with thirty-eight successful solutions, including one proof that provided an even more elegant solution than the one offered by Russell and Whitehead.

Although unenamored with the term "artificial intelligence" at first, Simon quickly came around. Recalling Logic Theorist in a later autobiography, Simon saw the program as a significant breakthrough in terms of both human and machine intelligence. "We invented a computer program capable of thinking non-numerically, and thereby solved the venerable mind/body problem, explaining how a system composed of matter can have the properties of mind."[5]

Despite later ego battles—Minsky claimed to have come up with many of the heuristic methods used by Newell and Simon but had moved on by the time of the conference[6]—Dartmouth would give birth to what A.I. historian Daniel Crevier describes as the "golden age" of the field. "After Dartmouth, A.I., for better or for worse, was now a field of intellectual inquiry," writes Crevier. "In many ways it was no more unified than it had been before 1956 but, perhaps because of the continuing exchange of ideas initiated at Dartmouth, A.I. started progressing by leaps and bounds."[7]

Researchers indeed showed rapid progress. At the Carnegie Institute (later Carnegie Mellon University) Newell and Simon quickly followed up Logic Theorist with an even more ambitious effort, dubbed General Problem Solver (GPS). In addition to writing proofs, including one geometric proof that had defied mathematicians for centuries, the program solved puzzles and word problems through a general technique known as means-ends analysis. At MIT, where Minsky and McCarthy had started a new laboratory dedicated solely to artificial intelligence, students combined McCarthy's newly developed LISP programming language—short for List Processing— with Simon and Newell's breakthroughs to create a range of expert-level programs. Among the most notable were Student, developed by Daniel G. Bobrow, which could solve algebra problems presented in sentence form, and DENDRAL, by Ed Feigenbaum, which could solve college freshman–level chemistry test problems.[8]

"I don't mean to shock you," wrote Simon to academic readers of a 1958 paper. "But the simplest way I can summarize is to say that there are now machines that think, that learn and that create. Moreover, their ability to do these things is going to increase rapidly until—in a visible future—the range of problems they can handle will be coextensive with the range to which the human mind has been applied."[9]

In that same paper, Simon went on to predict that, within the decade, researchers at Carnegie or some other institution would come out with machines that could defeat the world's chess champion, that could apply theories of human psychology, and that could solve an unproven math theorem. Given the speed with which GPS achieved the final prediction, those within the artificial-intelligence community had little reason to doubt the veracity of these claims.

Outside the field, however, the first signs of a backlash were starting to emerge. In 1960 British philosopher John R. Lucas fired the first salvo with the paper "Mind, Machines and Gödel." Pitting the A.I. field's two most prominent forefathers—Gödel and Turing— against each other, Lucas called Gödel's incompleteness theorem an Achilles' heel for artificial-intelligence systems. Formal logic and heuristic decision-making might work well when generating mathematical proofs or playing simple games such as checkers, but in the real world, such rule-based systems fell prey to paradoxical situations and inconsistencies. The human mind, on the other hand, possessed the ability to recognize and work around paradoxical traps, hinting at the presence of decision-making factors beyond the scope of formal logic [http://users.ox.ac.uk/~jrlucas/mmg.html]. "Thanks to Gödel's theorem, the mind always has the last word," wrote Lucas. "[It] can always go one better than any formal, ossified, dead system can." Although scientists vehemently disputed Lucas's conclusion, the scientific trend of the 1960s was a general movement away from logic and heuristics and toward systems that more closely modeled the innate and, at times, intuitive nature of human reasoning. Starting with McCarthy in the late 1950s, A.I. researchers became obsessed with the notion of *common sense*. Why was it, they wondered, that a computer program could solve collegiate-level chemistry questions and yet stumble unexpectedly when presented with questions even a five-year-old child could answer? Simple questions such as "Why can you pull a rope but not push one?" or "Do all birds fly?" led even the most sophisticated programs into a Möbius strip maze of analogy, definition, and counterdefinition [http://csel.cs.colorado.edu/~cs3202/papers/Muneeb_Cheema.html].

By the end of the 1960s, concern over the "brittle" nature of expert systems prompted leading researchers such as McCarthy and Minsky to espouse a more "connectionist" approach to A.I. The connectionist approach saw human intelligence as an assortment of decision-making processes as opposed to a single GPS-style decision tree. More and more, scientists were coming to view the brain as a "messy kludge" of mechanical subsystems masquerading as a single, integrated whole [www.ai.mit.edu/people/minsky/papers/SymbolicVs.Connectionist.txt].

When 1968 rolled around and Simon's prediction of a world-champion-level chess program had failed to develop, A.I. critics had more fuel for the fire. The chief critic to emerge in the mid-1960s was MIT professor Hubert Dreyfus. While working as a consultant at Rand, Dreyfus had penned a critical investigative report titled "Alchemy and Artificial Intelligence." Published in 1965, the report attracted the attention of the *New Yorker,* which mentioned it in its "Talk of the Town" section. Soon Dreyfus had a book deal. In 1972 he put out *What Computers Can't Do: A Critique of Artificial Reason.*

In the book's conclusion Dreyfus chastised researchers for letting human emotion influence scientific research. Instead of treating the computer as a knowledge-assisting tool, he maintained, A.I. researchers were seeing it as a canvas on which they could paint their own, unaided models of intelligence. "To avoid the fate of the alchemists, it is time we asked where we stand," Dreyfus wrote. "Is an exhaustive analysis of human reason into rule-governed operations on discrete, determinate, context-free elements possible? Is an approximation to this goal of artificial reason even probable? The answer to both these questions appears to be, No."

Dreyfus's comments would form the critical backdrop for A.I. research throughout the 1970s, a decade fraught with turmoil in the scientific community. Like the space program, A.I. research suffered in the wake of the Vietnam War. Most of the field's funding had come from the Defense Department, which hoped to reap the rewards through more intelligent weapons on the battlefield. By 1975, this funding was starting to wane, and A.I. researchers were turning to the private sector for funding. A growing number of companies founded by A.I. researchers sprang up in the late 1970s, selling expert systems and other A.I. technologies developed in the lab. In the mid-1980s, the Japanese government unveiled its "fifth-generation" project. The project, a joint effort of government and industry to speed the development of artificial intelligence technology for the commercial marketplace, elevated A.I. to the realm of corporate strategy and national security. American companies, already pressed by their Japanese competitors, had no choice but to follow suit. Soon Ford and General Motors were clamoring for expert systems to streamline manufacturing and procurement.

While scientists fought to keep their laboratories funded and their assistants from jumping to the private sector, the debate over A.I. took a dramatic turn in 1979. That year saw the publication of *Gödel, Escher, Bach: An Eternal Golden Braid,* a book written by itinerant math professor and classical-music fan Douglas Hofstadter.

Upon first glance, Hofstadter's Pulitzer Prize–winning book comes off as an extended, colorfully written riff on the theme of art and human creativity. Read more closely, however, it quickly reveals itself to be a continuation of the Gödel versus Turing debate launched by Lucas two decades before. In walking readers through the lengthy mathematical background of the A.I. field, Hofstadter repeatedly directs readers' attention to what he called "strange loops," music fugues, optical illusions, and self-defining statements such as Gödel's paradoxical "This statement cannot be proven." Instead of seeing Gödel's theorem as an Achilles' heel, Hofstadter holds it up as evidence of the self-reference that emerges within any sufficiently complex system. "Gödel's strange loop," wrote Hofstadter in 1999, "allows a system to 'perceive itself,' to talk about itself, to become 'self aware,' and in a sense it would not be going too far to say that, by virtue of having such a loop, a formal system acquires a 'self.' "[10]

Combining the automata theories of von Neumann with recent developments in A.I. research, Hofstadter painted ideas, hopes, and even consciousness itself as "emergent effects" brought out by the complex interplay between the mechanical subsystems of the human brain. Philosophers who had formerly relied upon Gödel's work as a proof of the brain's nonmechanical nature responded by zeroing in on the issue of machine consciousness. Dubbing Hofstadter's doctrinaire approach to consciousness the "strong A.I." thesis, they quickly cut it away from the main body of traditional, or "good old-fashioned," A.I.

Of all the counterattacks, the most famous was the essay "Minds, Brains and Programs," written by Berkeley philosophy professor John Searle. It outlines what has since become known as Searle's "Chinese room" argument. Searle's paper begins with a colorful twist on Turing's Imitation Game: Picture a person—in this case, Searle himself—locked inside a room. The person is given a large stack of questions written in Chinese and, although he knows no Chinese, must translate and respond to each question. Fortunately, there is a large manual that instructs the prisoner exactly how to answer each question. Over time, the prisoner gets so good that his answers become indistinguishable from those of a native Chinese speaker. In other words, Searle argues, the answers are intelligent enough to pass a Turing test—in Chinese no less!—even though the person sitting inside the room has done nothing but read directions in English and follow the rules given [http://members.aol.com/NeoNoetics/MindsBrainsPrograms.html]. "As far as the Chinese is concerned," writes Searle, "I behave like a computer."

Searle's conclusion: Although the character in the thought experiment is responding intelligently, the process giving rise to that output is fundamentally different from that of a native speaker responding to the same questions. At no time does the person following the instructions understand the information he is processing or recognize the people submitting the questions. Without comprehension or recognition, argues Searle, there can be no consciousness.

While not dismissing the possibility of artificial intelligence per se, Searle's critique would provide a solid defense against those who see the mind as little more than a software program riding atop the brain's biomechanical hardware. "No one would suppose that we could produce milk and sugar by running a computer simulation of the formal sequences in lactation and photosynthesis," writes Searle, "but where the mind is concerned many people are willing to believe in such a miracle."

Searle's arguments and the drifting nature of the A.I. debate prompted many A.I. researchers to accuse A.I. critics of "moving the goalposts." A growing number of researchers had already begun to view artificial intelligence as a field defined less by what computers could do than by what they couldn't do. "In biology, we demonstrate mutations in fruit flies and immediately conclude that, if one were clever enough, we could figure out what the millions of genes in humans do," groused Herbert Simon in a 1994 interview [www.omnimag.com/archives/interviews/simon.html]. "In A.I., the rule seems to be that when you tell somebody your computer plays pretty good chess, they say, 'But can it do hopscotch?' "

Regardless of where the goalposts stood, the A.I. research community's penchant for false prediction had already become a burden by the early 1980s. A brief burst in the number of companies offering commercial expert systems and the fifth-generation project helped keep A.I. in the media spotlight, but even before the A.I. companies went out of business and the Japanese effort evaporated, observers in the media and the business community were already questioning the field's unhealthy reputation for hype.

"The emperor—whether talking about the fifth generation or AI—is stark naked from the ankles up," wrote IBM engineer Herb Grosch in 1984. "From the ankles down, the emperor is wearing a well-worn and heavily gilded pair of shoes called expert systems. They are useful, but we've had them for over 30 years. All that the fifth-generation boys have done is relabel them."[11]

This "emperor's new clothes" theme would pop up again in the title of physicist Roger Penrose's 1989 book *The Emperor's New Mind*. Taking the A.I. debate back to its roots yet again, Penrose re-examined the theoretical perspectives of both Gödel and Turing in the context of postwar discoveries in the fields of molecular biology and quantum physics. Penrose's conclusion—that both quantum physics and relativity leave enough room for the brain to operate outside the bounds of mechanical computation—would take the debate back even further. Noting the importance of time in the mind's ability to sort out events, Penrose invokes the a priori arguments of Kant and Plato at book's end. "My guess is that there is something illusory here," Penrose writes. "The temporal ordering that we 'appear' to perceive is, I am claiming, something that we impose upon our perceptions in order to make sense of them in relation to the uniform forward time-progression of an external physical reality."[12]

Despite the increasingly esoteric nature of the A.I. debate—or maybe because of it—the last two decades have witnessed a digging-in process within the A.I. research community. While philosophers and physicists debate the nature of consciousness, free will, and the unidirectional passage of time, A.I. researchers seem more interested in breaking down the study of intelligence into a few narrow domains: language comprehension, machine vision, and automated learning systems. Many scientists, most notably MIT robotics researcher Rodney Brooks, see the Turing notion of building electronic brains as hopelessly outdated. Adopting the design mantra "fast, cheap and out of control," Brooks and his followers have focused on insectlike robots with a few simple built-in intelligence processes in the hopes that their behavior will adapt and evolve into more complex, and more intelligent, designs.

In a 1997 review of *HAL's Legacy: 2001's Computer as Dream and Reality* [www.sciam.com/0197issue/0197review2.html], a book edited by David Stork, *Scientific American* staff writer Paul Wallich summed up the trend: "In the subsequent A.I. winter—brought on by the end of a military research spree as well as the inevitable collision between venture capital and reality—only the mechanical cockroaches survived. Researchers scaled back their ambitions and aimed at achieving the cognitive and survival skills of a lobster or a cricket rather than a virtuoso surgeon or an ace fighter pilot."

Such scaling back, however, has helped raise the profile of projects that retain a glimmer of the early Turing-inspired ambition. Chief among these projects is Cyc, a thirty-year effort to build a comprehensive encyclopedia for artificial-intelligence systems. Launched by former Stanford professor Doug Lenat in 1983, the project began with a goal to assemble 2 million independent facts and let Cyc build its internal intelligence through linking and inductive logic. Since then, Lenat and his colleagues have raised the target to 20 million facts, attracting $50 million in funding from the Defense Department and high-profile investors such as Microsoft cofounder Paul Allen. Although some critics have held up Cyc as the ultimate A.I. boondoggle, the effort seems to be paying off. In a June 1998 test, Cyc outscored all other knowledge bases combined when Pentagon scientists fed it three hundred pages of raw data and subjected the program to a barrage of commonsense questions [www.latimes.com/business/20010621/t000051293.html].

From the perspective of traditional A.I. research, the last decade of the twentieth century has proved to be a period of quiet vindication. The technological feats of the 1991 Gulf War demonstrated the growing power of intelligent weapons, while at the same time validating years of Defense Department–funded software research. The rapid emergence of the World Wide Web during the middle of the decade offered new market opportunities. Many commercial A.I. programs that had been on the ropes at the beginning of the decade gained new life as search engines and autonomous "agents," programs that assisted novice Web users in their struggle to keep up with the exploding new medium.

The most dramatic A.I. event of the decade, however, would occur in 1997 when Deep Blue, an IBM computer running a chess program with heuristic search algorithms dating back to Simon and Newell's GPS, defeated world chess champion Garry Kasparov in a six-game match [www.research.ibm.com/deepblue/home/html/b.html].

Afterward, Dreyfus, Kasparov technical adviser Frederic Friedel, and Daniel Dennett, a professor of philosophy at Tufts, debated the significance of the match on *NewsHour with Jim Lehrer* [www.pbs. org/newshour/bb/entertainment/jan-june97/big_blue_5-12.html]. For Dreyfus, whose own loss to an MIT chess program in the late 1960s provided one of the signature triumphs of the field in its early days, Deep Blue's victory was yet another humbling moment. Still, Dreyfus challenged its long-term implications. "What this shows," Dreyfus said, "is in a world in which calculation is possible, [using] brute force meaningless calculation, the computer will always beat people, but when—in a world in which relevance and intelligence play a crucial role, the computer has always behaved miserably, and there's no reason to think that that will change with this victory."

For Dennett, author of the 1991 book *Consciousness Explained* and a leading exponent of the "strong A.I." school, Dreyfus's denigration of Deep Blue's achievements as the result of "brute force" calculation represented yet another example of A.I. critics "moving the goalposts." "The idea that there's something special about human intuition that is not capturable in the computer program is a sort of illusion," Dennett said. "I think, when people talk about intuition, it's just because they don't know how something's done. If we didn't know how Deep Blue did what it did, we'd be very impressed with its intuitive powers."

Despite such attempts to fold the Deep Blue victory into existing interpretations of artificial intelligence, the night's most insightful commentary belonged to Friedel, who, in summing up Kasparov's own reaction to the machine, provided fodder for future debate.

"When Gary [*sic*] Kasparov plays against the computer, he has the feeling that it is forming plans; it understands strategy; it's trying to trick him; it's blocking his ideas, and then to tell him, now, this has nothing to do with intelligence, it's just number crunching, seems very semantic to him. He says the performance is what counts. I see it behaves like something that's intelligent. If you put—if you put a curtain up, he plays the game and then you open the curtain, and it's a human being. He says, ah, that was intelligent, and if it's a box, he says, no, that was just number crunching. It's the performance he's interested in."

Since Deep Blue's victory, speculation over A.I. has increased significantly. A brief glance at the growing number of A.I.-themed books and articles with ominous titles—*The Age of Spiritual Machines,* "Robot Terror," *March of the Machines: Why the New Race of Robots Will Rule the World,* etc.—reflects a renewed fascination for what has quietly become an old field of science.

Looking back through the lens of a half century, John McCarthy, the man who was there at the beginning, gives a bemused laugh. While significant from a public relations perspective, programs such as Deep Blue come nowhere near fulfilling the A.I. vision initially laid out by McCarthy and other early pioneers. Although hope remains for future progress, the last fifty years can be viewed only as a disappointment.

"I was really quite optimistic about what might happen at Dartmouth," McCarthy says. "I somehow thought that getting this group of people working together would produce great results. As it happened, they didn't work together and it wouldn't have done any good if they had, because they didn't have good enough ideas."

McCarthy isn't the only one to use this argument. In his introduction to the 1985 book *Robotics,* McCarthy's former research partner Marvin Minsky blames most of the A.I. field's past troubles on ideas that were easy to come up with but hard to test. "If it takes a quarter of a century to test an idea—or to find out that it wasn't so good at all—then how long may it take to make sure machines are truly intelligent?" wonders Minsky. "If we need twenty such ideas, and each one has to be developed on the basis of the last, then the process could take five hundred years."[13]

McCarthy, for one, has always considered five hundred years to be a reasonable estimate. "Then again," he says, "maybe some graduate student has decided that McCarthy is all wrong and maybe that student is solving the problem. The breakthrough could come this year or next year."

What McCarthy doesn't believe is that artificial intelligence will simply emerge out of the technology ether. Citing recent books by Ray Kurzweil (*The Age of Spiritual Machines*) and Hans Moravec (*Robot*), as well as the April 2000 *Wired* magazine cover story by Bill Joy, McCarthy says the current rate of speculation is outpacing the rate of A.I. research by a wide margin. "Guys like Kurzweil and Moravec and maybe Bill Joy somehow think that you can take Moore's Law and project things into the future and say that, by 2020, you'll have human-level intelligence," McCarthy says. "I don't believe that at all. I think new ideas are required."

For McCarthy, the current wave of speculation inspires feelings of dèjá vu. During the final months of World War II, he says, journalists poured out fantastic predictions about the coming postwar period. Like his own predictions for the A.I. field, those of the journalists quickly fell flat as short-term trends met long-term realities. If the last half-century has taught us anything, McCarthy says, it's that you can't plot the future with a straight-edge ruler.

"One of the things they said was going to happen was that everyone was going to have their own helicopter," says McCarthy. "They were basing the prediction on the fact that you had all these people who were spending ten to twelve hours a day working on war projects. I guess if people did keep up that rate of productivity, personal helicopters would have been a cinch. But as history shows, the extrapolation didn't hold."

Chapter 3

—

THE OPTIMIST: RAY KURZWEIL

Standing in the cavernous backstage area of New York's Madison Square Garden, Ray Kurzweil, the founder and chief executive officer of Kurzweil Technologies, shifts his weight, checks his watch, and waits for the signal to step onstage.

The keynote speaker for the 2001 New York Music and Internet Expo, Kurzweil silently runs through the mental preparations for his upcoming speech. The expo organizers have promised a mind-blowing experience, and Kurzweil, no stranger to hype, appears un-fazed by the promise. Dressed in standard-issue CEO black—black slacks, black jacket, black polo shirt, no tie—he exudes the confidence and sartorial taste of a youthful minister or rabbi hungry to deliver a sermon.

Religious analogies are common in the high-tech world. In an in-dustry where uncertainty over products' long-term future can be alle-viated only through devout professions of consumer allegiance, stories about Macintosh "evangelists" and Microsoft Windows "faithful" engaging in chat-room "holy wars" are legion. Still, watching Kurzweil prepare for a speech, it's hard not to sense a legitimate piety. An author whose latest book title reads like something off the local church bulletin board—*The Age of Spiritual Machines: When Computers Exceed Human Intelligence*—Kurzweil clearly has no problem discussing the apocalyptic implications of modern technology. The title of his upcoming book, *The Singularity Is Near,* takes the theme of techno-rapture even further, hammering home the belief that technology is leading us all toward Something Better.

"The pace of change is accelerating," Kurzweil says, launching into his speech after the introductory panel cedes the stage. "The kind of change we've seen in the last thirty years we're going to see in the next five years. The kind of change we've seen over the last hundred years, we're going to see over the next twenty-five years. Over the next few minutes, I'd like to show you a few harbingers of that future."

With that, the lights dim.

——

For Raymond Kurzweil, the long journey up the exponential curve of modern technological progress began in 1948. Born and raised in Queens, New York, Kurzweil spent his childhood years tinkering with musical instruments and scavenging local shops for second-hand electronic equipment. Once, after stumbling upon a collection of telephone relays—devices used to build the logic circuits in early computers—Kurzweil assembled his first "computerlike" device for a junior high school science fair. A summer job at NYU led to software-programming experience, and at the age of fifteen, Kurzweil built a newer, more ambitious device with the power to recognize musical patterns and rework them into its own original compositions. The invention earned its creator a guest appearance on the 1960s game show *I've Got a Secret,* where Kurzweil played a sample composition on the piano, along with an invitation to the White House, as one of forty finalists in the Westinghouse Talent Search.[1]

It wasn't long before the top schools beckoned. Kurzweil chose MIT and, as a college student, rubbed elbows with many of the marquee names in computer science. Foremost was A.I. lab director Marvin Minsky, a man Kurzweil describes as a "generous teacher" and a lifelong friend. While at MIT, Kurzweil exhibited the entrepreneurial streak that would shape his future career. As a sophomore, he wrote a college-selection software program for high school students. The program was good enough to gain the attention of New York publisher Harcourt, Brace & World, which paid Kurzweil and his business partners $100,000 for the program.

Following MIT, Kurzweil's combined entrepreneurial and scientific interests led him deeper into the study of pattern recognition, a subdomain of A.I. offering numerous commercial opportunities. Starting with text-reading systems (Kurzweil Computer Products, Inc.) and moving on to musical synthesizers (Kurzweil Music Systems, Inc.) and voice-to-text conversion (Kurzweil Applied Intelligence, Inc.), Kurzweil quickly built up a reputation as a go-getter in a field better known for spinning its wheels.

It is a reputation Kurzweil has done his best to cultivate. Visitors to his on-line résumé at Kurzweiltech.com [www.kurzweiltech. com/raycv.htm] will come across a list of twelve technological "firsts," not to mention a list of the seven companies founded—and, on occasion, sold to larger companies—by Kurzweil.

"Ray's definitely a can-do guy," says Ken Linde, senior Web architect for Kurzweil's latest venture, Kurzweil Technologies, Inc. "He'll sit down in a meeting, explain what he wants and why it will work according to plan. There's always this positive attitude, which, believe it or not, can be a rare thing in the high-tech industry."

For the first twenty years of his career, Kurzweil was willing to be unique, letting others point out the numerous obstacles while he and his engineering crew went off to bag a few quick peaks. Sometime during the late 1980s, however, he began feeling a need to let others in on the positive attitude fueling his work. The result was his first book, *The Age of Intelligent Machines*. Published in 1990, it stands out among A.I. history books not only for its encyclopedic approach to the history of A.I. but also for its attempt to provide predictions on where that science might be heading in the coming decade.

Looking back, Kurzweil describes *The Age of Intelligent Machines* as an attempt to impart some of the wisdom and information gained during a career as a high-tech market watcher. "Being a high-tech entrepreneur is like being a surfer," he says. "You have to ride the wave at exactly the right time. You have to have some idea of where things are going. If your project's going to take three years, you want it to be relevant when it comes out. If it's ahead of its time, it won't be affordable. If it's behind its time, you'll be the eighteenth person out in the field."

In the course of developing his wave-catching skills, Kurzweil says, he became a committed fan of statistical modeling. Inspired by Intel cofounder Gordon Moore, whose 1965 observation that transistor density was increasing at an exponential rate has become an industry axiom, Kurzweil began working up charts and graphs in the hopes of identifying other hidden trends in the marketplace. After a decade of building models to brief investors, Kurzweil says, the hobby "took on a life of its own," prompting him to create a book on the future of technology, particularly the future of A.I.-related technology.

As books go, *The Age of Intelligent Machines* is a fairly sober attempt to school the entry-level reader on the science, philosophy, and politics of artificial intelligence. Mixing history and state-of-the-art research and tossing in enough pictures and graphs to keep the nontechnical reader at ease, Kurzweil successfully walks the tightrope between rampant hype and withering skepticism. When Kurzweil does look into the future, he makes sure to limit his predictions to the coming decade. In addition to anticipating the arrival of a "worldwide computer network" and the strategic use of intelligent weapons in warfare—predictions fulfilled by the Internet and the Gulf War—Kurzweil went out on a limb, speculating that in 1998 we would see the defeat of a human chess champion by a computer chess program.

Of all the predictions, the chess prediction allowed the least amount of wiggle room. In making it, Kurzweil plotted the rate of progress among computer chess programs since Simon and

Newell's first release of General Problem Solver in the late 1950s. Noting that computer chess rankings have been improving along an exponential curve, Kurzweil simply extended the curve until it crossed the Chess Federation's 2,800-point threshold, a ranking level occupied by top players, such as Boris Spassky, Bobby Fischer, and Garry Kasparov.

As fate would have it, Kurzweil's extrapolation exercise missed Deep Blue's 1997 victory by a full year. Still, even with a twelve-month error, the guess was accurate enough to motivate a follow-up book, and by the end of the year, Kurzweil was already working on it.

During the eight-year period between artificial-intelligence books, Kurzweil's optimism seems to have followed its own exponential growth trajectory. In 1992 Kurzweil penned *The 10% Solution for a Healthy Life,* a book documenting a personal battle against type II diabetes, a disease that Kurzweil claims to have beaten through improved diet and exercise. Increasingly fascinated with issues of longevity and consciousness, Kurzweil began examining the science of artificial intelligence from the long-term perspective. Convinced that the A.I. threshold of intelligent machines had already been crossed, Kurzweil elected to give his follow-up book a more ambitious title: *The Age of Spiritual Machines.*

"The accelerating pace of change is inexorable," writes Kurzweil in the book's epilogue. "The emergence of machines that exceed human intelligence in all of its broad diversity is inevitable. But we still have the power to shape our future technology, and our future lives. That is the main reason I wrote this book."[2]

———

For the purposes of the New York Music and Internet Expo, Kurzweil is concerned less with predicting the future than with giving his fellow innovators a brief taste of it. Today's keynote speech represents the East Coast debut of Ramona, a software entity created by Kurzweil and his fellow engineers at Kurzweil Technologies.

The presentation begins with an overhead screen flashing the computer-generated image of a human face. At first glance the face looks to be a mixture of Deborah Harry, lead singer of the new-wave group Blondie, and Lara Croft, virtual star of the recent best-selling video game Tomb Raider. Upon closer inspection, however, the face proves to be an animated computer representation of an anonymous human model.

As Kurzweil and an assistant run through a vocal-calibration exercise, the face swivels to and fro, much like an eager guest on the television show *Nightline.* The swivel movement is rhythmic, a bit too rhythmic almost, and as the calibration wears on, the programmed nature of the seemingly random movement becomes apparent.

"I'm sorry for the delay, folks," says Kurzweil, acknowledging the length of time it takes the voice-recognition system—a technology Kurzweil helped develop in the early 1990s—to recognize his voice amid the background hum.

When the calibration is complete, Kurzweil stares up at the computer-generated image and fires off a question.

"Who are you?"

After a pause, Kurzweil's words appear in an on-screen box adjacent to the Ramona image. For a second, it seems as if the computer is on the verge of crashing—until, suddenly, rolling text fills the screen. "I'm Ramona," it reads.

"I'm Ramona," the image says, echoing the text. "I am Ray Kurzweil's twenty-five-year-old female alter ego. I'm also the host of KurzweilAI.net. So like a friend of mine once said, 'Why don't you come up and see me sometime?' "

The image stops speaking, followed by a brief moment of awkward silence, followed by a rolling wave of laughter from the audience. The voice is Kurzweil's own, doctored slightly to match the frequency range of an adult female. Its mechanical lilt betrays the presence of yet another software program, this time a text-to-voice converter running algorithms first developed by Kurzweil and his engineering team in the late 1970s.

It's hard to tell what's grabbing the audience's collective funny bone. Is it the Mae West line or the appearance of Kurzweil in computer-generated drag? Perhaps it's the sheer awkwardness of the Ramona character's on-screen presence. After years of experiencing autonomous androids in the form of affable movie characters—Arnold Schwarzenegger's Terminator, Anthony Daniels's C-3PO, and Brent Spiner's Data—encountering a true to life example can be a jarring experience.

Perhaps sensing the awkwardness, Kurzweil fires off another quick question. "What is virtual reality?" he asks, looking down at his feet.

"Virtual reality is where you can find me," answers Ramona, reading from an already visible paragraph. "It is a place where you can be anything you want to be and go anywhere you want to go."

The interview continues like this for another five minutes, Kurzweil throwing a succession of basic questions at his virtual creation and Ramona running through a list of answers that seem half scripted, half assembled from basic facts and flirtatious quips. While not exactly a Turing test, the repartee provides evidence that Ramona is responding autonomously when the voice-to-text converter bungles a few incoming questions. When this happens, gibberish fills the text box on the screen. Rather than answer, Ramona remains silent, waiting for a proper question to come out of Kurzweil's lips.

·Billed as a "virtual blow-up doll" by one technology publication, Ramona is in fact a fairly impressive repository of state-of-the-art interactive-software technologies. Fusing three-dimensional computer animation with voice-to-text and text-to-voice conversion software and backing it all with a sophisticated knowledge base able to interpret simple questions, including the existentially challenging "Who are you?" Ramona offers a perfect example of the jigsaw-puzzle nature of artificial intelligence. Sure, some of the movements are clunky and the responses stilted, but taken as a whole, it's an impressive performance.

Indeed, watching Ramona speak, and watching the crowd react to her comments, one quickly gets a sense of the performance aspect that goes into any conversation. Since the 1960s, A.I. researchers have recognized the human capacity for emotional "projection" and have exploited it as a shortcut to passing the Turing test. To date, the best example of this exploitation is ELIZA, a conversational program written by MIT professor Joseph Weizenbaum in 1965. Posing as a Rogerian psychologist, ELIZA tricked unsuspecting users into pouring out their hearts, simply by focusing on a few psychologically significant keywords and fashioning responses designed to draw out the conversation.

In his 1966 paper documenting the experiment, Weizenbaum published a snippet of typical ELIZA-"patient" dialogue [http://acf5.nyu.edu/~mm64/x52.9265/january1966.html]:

USER: Men are all alike.

ELIZA: IN WHAT WAY?

USER: They're always bugging us about something or other.

ELIZA: CAN YOU THINK OF A SPECIFIC EXAMPLE?

USER: Well, my boyfriend made me come here.

ELIZA: YOUR BOYFRIEND MADE YOU COME HERE

USER: He says I'm depressed much of the time.

ELIZA: I AM SORRY TO HEAR YOU ARE DEPRESSED

USER: It's true. I am unhappy

ELIZA: DO YOU THINK COMING HERE WILL HELP YOU NOT TO BE UN-HAPPY

USER: I need some help, that much seems certain.

ELIZA: WHAT WOULD IT MEAN TO YOU IF YOU GOT SOME HELP

USER: Perhaps I could learn to get along with my mother.

ELIZA: TELL ME MORE ABOUT YOUR FAMILY[3]

"ELIZA performs best when its human correspondent is initially instructed to 'talk' to it, via the typewriter of course, just as one would to a psychiatrist," summarized Weizenbaum. "This mode of conversation was chosen because the psychiatric interview is one of the few examples of categorized dyadic natural language communication in which one of the participating pair is free to assume the pose of knowing almost nothing of the real world."

—

While there certainly are a number of ELIZA-esque elements to Ramona—the name itself seems to hint at an homage—the Kurzweil-Ramona dialogue goes beyond the coy thrust and parry of Eliza and other offshoot chatterbot programs. Like Pinocchio dancing without strings, Ramona's ability to parse sentences and construct answers from deep within her silicon brain is impressive enough to keep the hecklers at bay. And though Kurzweil never opens the demo to questions from the floor, one gets the sense that, if given the chance, they'd probably direct their questions to Ramona in the same respectful tones reserved for talking with a fellow human.

As if to drive this point home, Kurzweil throws in a final question about "common sense," the blanket term most A.I. researchers use to refer to the last great terra incognita of human intelligence.

"This makes me think of something Marvin Minsky once said," Ramona answers, "'Deep Blue may be able to win at chess, but it does not know to come in from the rain.' Well, here in virtual reality, it only rains when you want it to. Anyway, I have to say common sense is one of those ways in which humans are still more advanced than computers. But then again, I've seen some humans do some pretty dumb things."

Yet another ripple of laughter rolls through the crowd.

—

If *The Age of Intelligent Machines* offered a sober commentary on the present course of artificial intelligence circa 1990, *The Age of Spiritual Machines* introduces readers to a much more wide-open vision of the future. Enclosed within its pages is the implicit message that artificial intelligence is not only possible but inevitable. Using statistics as his guide, Kurzweil attempts to forge the link between human and technological evolution, presenting them as two sides of the same coin. In one chapter subheading, Kurzweil succinctly sums up the linkage: "Technology: A continuation of evolution by other means."

Since the book's publication, events such as the New York Music and Internet Expo keynote speech have become forums for Kurzweil to expand upon this dual vision. Instead of driving home the evolutionary nature of modern design, Kurzweil prefers to zero in on the phenomenon of what he calls "double exponential" growth. The term is a reference to a chart published in *The Age of Spiritual Machines*. In it, Kurzweil outlines the rate of computer evolution in terms of computational speed per unit cost, as opposed to the usual Moore's Law metric, transistor density. As a result, Kurzweil is free to extend his data points outward, including mechanical devices such as the 1908 Hollerith Tabulator and the 1911 Monroe Calculator. These devices don't qualify as computers under the modern definition, but they did perform calculations, a fact that gives Kurzweil the opportunity to compare their performance with that of modern computers on a calculations-per-second basis.

The curve generated by Kurzweil's new data set is illuminating. It mimics the usual upward-arcing trajectory of most technology curves, but with one notable exception. When Kurzweil plots the data points on a logarithmic scale—that is, when he replaces the numbers on the vertical axis with exponential values of 10—the curve's upward-arcing nature still remains intact. In other words, not only have computational speeds increased at an exponential rate over the last century, but the rate of that increase is also increasing over time.

Having examined this unusual trajectory over the last two decades, Kurzweil offers an explanation: Moore's Law, while dramatic, is just one trend reflecting the rate of innovation. In fact, it is the last of what Kurzweil considers five major trends that have shaped computer evolution over the last century. As successive trends have stacked up, one on top of the other, the exponential rate of improvement in modern computer systems has received a series of periodic upward nudges, resulting in so-called double-exponential growth.

"If you look at the history of technology, you will notice a cascade of S-curves, one arriving on top of [the] other," says Kurzweil after the morning speech, rubbing a gold Mickey Mouse wristwatch. "First you get slow growth, then you get explosive growth, and then you get slow growth again as physical limitations are met. Moore's Law is just one of many paradigms."

Although Kurzweil says he built the double-exponential growth model two decades ago, *The Age of Intelligent Machines* makes only indirect reference to the Moore's Law phenomenon. It would take an additional decade's worth of research and plugging in data points to push Kurzweil into giving Moore's Law a central role in his new book.[4]

In the course of collecting those data points, Kurzweil has become more convinced that the current rate of technological acceleration is more than just a momentary phenomenon. Indeed, just as the shape of a nautilus shell betrays the existence of underlying mathematical algorithms,[5] the radically accelerating nature of technology is a sign of evolution's own predisposition toward increasingly intelligent design.

"The emergence of technology was a milestone in the evolution of intelligence on Earth because it represented a new means of evolution recording its designs," writes Kurzweil in *The Age of Spiritual Machines*. "The next milestone will be technology creating its own next generation without human intervention. That there is only a period of tens of thousands of years between these two milestones is another example of the exponentially quickening pace that is evolution."

In other words, trace the overall arc of computer innovation and it isn't hard to see where it's heading: The human brain holds about 100 billion neurons, with each neuron possessing roughly 1,000 connections, each capable of simultaneous activity. Throw it all together, Kurzweil says, and you have a device with phenomenal power—20 quadrillion calculations per second, assuming that each neuron fires 200 times per second—yet little or no improvement from one generation to the next. Compare that with today's average

$1,000 computer system, a device that currently operates at 1 billion calculations per second but whose performance level is expected to increase 8,000-fold over the next twenty years, provided Moore's Law doesn't run into unforeseen quantum-miniaturization barriers. Even without Moore's Law, scientists are already working with supercomputer systems built out of common off-the-shelf PC systems wired together and run in parallel, like the neurons of the brain itself.[6] In either case, you've got a repeat of the computer-chess curve in the early 1990s: Given enough time, enough growth in processing power, and the occasional radical design breakthrough, Kurzweil says, it won't be long before ordinary computers achieve the computational speed and complexity of the human brain. "The amount of unused computation on the Internet today exceeds the computational capacity of the human brain," argues Kurzweil. "Supercomputers will reach the 20-million-billion-calculations-per-second capacity of the human brain around 2010, a decade earlier than personal computers."

So what then? Is computational speed and complexity enough to drive artificial intelligence? Kurzweil thinks so, pointing to both Deep Blue and Turing's groundbreaking paper "On Computable Numbers." Replace Turing's fanciful logical computing machine with a worldwide network of high-speed computers—each built according to Turing-machine specifications—and you have the makings of a true universal machine, a device that replicates the performance of any other mechanical device, including the human brain.

Not everybody buys into this view, of course. On the one side you have theologians and philosophers who refuse to accept that the human mind is simply data being shuttled around a biochemical machine—the brain. On the other side, you have more than a few A.I. researchers who disagree with the notion that computer evolution is a self-directed process, since such a view relegates today's A.I. research efforts to a mere handmaiden role in the evolutionary process. Quips one prominent researcher, "With friends like Ray Kurzweil, who needs enemies?"

Such criticism, however, has done little to diminish Kurzweil's ardor. The list of predictions in *The Age of Spiritual Machines* is audacious to say the least: downloadable thoughts by 2029, bodiless beings by 2099. Since the book's publication, Kurzweil has become even more obsessed with the notion of high-speed growth. The theme is central to his planned next book, entitled *The Singularity Is Near.* Likening the current acceleration of computer technology to the acceleration of gravity near a black hole—the term "singularity" is used by astrophysicists to describe the region of infinite density within a black hole—Kurzweil says human society is rapidly approaching the evolutionary equivalent of an event horizon, i.e., a point of no return. "As exponential growth continues to accelerate into the first half of the twenty-first century, it will appear to explode into infinity, at least from the limited and linear perspective of contemporary humans," writes Kurzweil in an introductory on-line précis to the book. "The progress will ultimately become so fast that it will rupture our ability to follow it. It will literally get out of our control. The illusion that we have our hand 'on the plug' will be dispelled."[7]

Kurzweil isn't the first author to run exponential growth curves out to their inevitable—or absurd—end points. His use of the term "singularity" is a direct reference to an essay by science-fiction author and San Diego State University math professor Vernor Vinge. Published in 1993, Vinge's essay stresses many of the same themes: hyper growth, hyper connectivity, and the emergence of an as yet undefinable superintelligence.[8] Since the publication of "What Is the Singularity?" the notion of human and machine intelligence fusing to create a new form of superintelligence has popped up in a number of books, such as *Out of Control,* by *Wired* magazine editor Kevin Kelly; *Darwin Among the Machines,* by George Dyson; and *The Spike: How Our Lives Are Being Transformed by Rapidly Advancing Technologies,* by Damien Broderick.

Even within the A.I. world, Kurzweil's perspective is far from unique. Both *The Age of Intelligent Machines* and *The Age of Spiritual Machines* draw inspiration from the 1988 book *Mind Children,* written by Carnegie Mellon robotics researcher Hans Moravec [www.frc.ri.cmu.edu/~hpm/]. Moravec's follow-up book, *Robot: From Mere Machine to Transcendent Mind,* came out concurrently with *The Age of Spiritual Machines,* making the two authors a popular tandem for future-oriented conferences and scientific panels. Kurzweil also appears to draw inspiration from the predictions of A.I. pioneer Marvin Minsky, whose 1994 *Scientific American* essay "Will Robots Inherit the Earth?" examines many of the evolutionary issues at the core of *The Age of Spiritual Machines* [www.ai.mit. edu/people/minsky/papers/sciam.inherit.txt]. Writes Minsky, "In the past, we have tended to see ourselves as a final product of evolution—but our evolution has not ceased. Indeed, we are now evolving more rapidly—although not in the familiar, slow Darwinian way. It is time that we started to think about our new emerging identities."

Where Kurzweil does stand out is in his "been there, built that" track record. Free of the politics of academia and immune to charges of carpetbagging, Kurzweil's conclusions come from a range of experience most traditional A.I. critics have a hard time confronting. "When you see Moravec speak, or when you interview him, you encounter a socially awkward, solitary man whose love of robots and comfort with the obsolescence of us becomes very understandable," says Erik Davis, author of the 1998 book *Techgnosis.* "Kurzweil, on the other hand, is a slickster, and he has a much wider mainstream audience than any of these people, partly because of his predictive success, partly because of his packaging, and partly because he's on to something."

Even potential allies have scratched their heads at times. Douglas Hofstadter, the author of the A.I. classic *Gödel, Escher, Bach,* says he accepts the notion that artificial intelligence is advancing faster than most people think. Still, he also admits to feeling concern over the credulous tone conveyed by books such as *The Age of Spiritual Machines* and *Robot.* "My gut-level instinct when I read both of these books is that I don't trust this," says Hofstadter. "There's a degree of scientific thinking mixed with mystical yearnings that makes me a little uncomfortable."

Kurzweil, for one, doesn't deny the mystical overtones of his latest book. Nor does he lament the diminished comfort level of those A.I. researchers who retain hope for a more heroic role in the evolution of artificial intelligence. If anything, he says, books such as *Robot* and *The Age of Spiritual Machines* have helped the A.I. community by reinstilling the sense of open-ended possibility felt by original pioneers such as McCarthy, Simon, and Minsky. "I think the momentum is back," he says. "I'm not the only person making these kinds of predictions. There's a community and a movement."

Given the failures of past predictions, Kurzweil says, it's understandable that some A.I. researchers have become a little gun-shy over the last two decades. Then again, if researchers spent less time in the laboratory and more time on the front lines, building technologies directly for the commercial marketplace, they'd see the greater risks associated with trying to put a theoretical box around technological evolution.

"All those overly optimistic predictions from thirty years ago are water over the dam," Kurzweil says. "We have a much more sophisticated understanding of what's required now. We know more about the brain, and we're learning more with every passing year."

As for the reception of audiences to his books, not to mention live performances such as his recently completed duet with Ramona, Kurzweil says he couldn't be more pleased. Most audience members are lay people who, perhaps even more than their academic and professional peers, have experienced the jarring effects of technological innovation. "The pace is accelerating and the public can feel it. It's affecting our lives. People now use cell phones and ATMs, and have access to all these different communications modalities. When I grew up there were only three television channels. Now there are hundreds. The rate of change is getting faster, and it's all because of technology. People can see this with their own eyes. They can taste it."

Chapter 4

—

THE HUMANIST: JARON LANIER

Maybe it's the hair—white-boy dreadlocks and an unkempt Pan-like goatee. Or the eyes—so blue they seem to occupy their own niche of the visible light spectrum. Maybe it's the paradoxical combination of Old World insouciance and New World optimism. Whatever it is, nearly two decades after bursting onto the high-tech scene—and spawning a generation of cliché-worthy pretenders in the process—Jaron Lanier still exudes the aura of an enfant terrible.

Best known for his pioneering work in virtual reality, a field of computer science he helped name as well as create, Lanier has built a career characterized by tireless deviation from the mean. Whether battling mutinous investors, "zombie" philosophers, or "good old-fashioned" A.I. researchers, Lanier rarely passes up the opportunity for a good fight.

"For the last twenty years, I have found myself on the inside of a revolution, but on the outside of its resplendent dogma," writes Lanier, introducing himself to readers in a November 2000 *Wired* magazine essay [www.wired.com/wired/archive/8.12/lanier.html].

"Now that the revolution has not only hit the mainstream, but bludgeoned it into submission by taking over the economy, it's probably time to cry out my dissent more loudly than I have before." Titled "One-Half of a Manifesto: Why Stupid Software Will Save the Future from Darwinian Machines," Lanier's essay is aimed squarely at the future fetishism of Ray Kurzweil, Hans Moravec, and, to a lesser degree, fellow software developer Bill Joy.

Instead of calling his opponents "extropian" or "transhumanist," blanket terms the media have applied to the writing of Kurzweil, Moravec, et al., Lanier prefers his own term: cybernetic totalism. The first half of "One-Half of a Manifesto" is devoted to laying out what Lanier considers the core tenets of the cybernetic-totalist philosophy: the belief that all living phenomena can be boiled down to mechanical or cybernetic processes; that "subjective experience"—or individual consciousness—is only a mirage; that the same Darwinistic forces driving biological evolution are driving technological evolution; and, finally, that current rates of technological evolution are pushing the entire *Homo sapiens* species to the brink of a major evolutionary breakthrough—or cataclysm, depending on your point of view.

"The dogma I object to is composed of a set of interlocking beliefs," writes Lanier. "It has the potential to transform human experience more powerfully than any prior ideology, religion, or political system ever has, partly because it can be so pleasing to the mind, at least initially, but mostly because it gets a free ride on the overwhelmingly powerful technologies that happen to be created by people who are, to a large degree, true believers."

Such literary shuffling is merely a setup for the uppercut Lanier saves for the A.I. research camp. Echoing Hubert Dreyfus, the author who once likened A.I. research to alchemy, Lanier accuses the A.I. research camp and its followers of putting faith before scientific skepticism. Lanier likens the current fascination with A.I. to medieval scholars' attempts to prove the existence of God through Aristotelian logic. In their haste to endorse the concept of thinking machines, many authors are putting scientific faith before scientific skepticism. "I'm hoping the reader can see that artificial intelligence is better understood as a belief system instead of a technology," he writes.

—

Seated in the back of a Tribeca coffee shop, Jaron Lanier munches on a breakfast croissant and mulls over his sudden position at the head of the anti-A.I. camp. "I have mixed feelings about it, really," he admits. "I've talked with [John] Searle a few times and I've sat on panels with other critics, and I have to say: I honestly find myself cringing at times when I listen to them. I always feel like their counterarguments are technically naïve or a little sloppy. It's like I want to root for my team, but they keep screwing up."

"One-Half of a Manifesto" is far from Lanier's first literary swipe at the A.I. camp or its allies. In fact, the essay culminates a five-year-long literary battle waged between Lanier and his opponents in Internet chat rooms and obscure publications such as the *Journal of Consciousness Studies*. Triggered by the publication of Daniel Dennett's 1991 book *Consciousness Explained*, the battle didn't boil over to the mainstream media until the spring of 2000.

"What happened was a German newspaper, *FAZ—Frankfurter Allgemeine Zeitung*—asked me to just write a piece, and [literary agent] John Brockman posted it on his website," says Lanier, sweeping a trademark dreadlock off his shoulder [www.edge.org]. "I think the original German version had a different title. Brockman said, Write me a column based on it. It wasn't so much about Kurzweil, but David Gelertner had just published a manifesto; so I said I wanted to write a manifesto, too. Unfortunately, a full manifesto would have required promoting all this other stuff, and I just wanted to point out a particular philosophy I saw emerging, so I decided to call it one-half of a manifesto. Then *Wired* picked it up, and now it's turned into this thing."

Although the essay drew strong reader responses, most of the participants in the ongoing debate over artificial intelligence seem to have greeted it with little more than a shrug. Kurzweil says he plans to address the essay in a future essay of his own but for the moment dismisses it as "myopic." Even A.I. critics find Lanier's piece hard to categorize. After reading through the essay for the first time, Dreyfus, an expected sympathizer, expresses bafflement. "Unfortunately, he has no argument," says Dreyfus, "and so I don't find it any more interesting than the views he rejects."[1]

Lanier, for one, acknowledges the incomplete nature of "One-Half of a Manifesto," both in the title and in his own descriptions of the work. As for lack of an argument, Lanier asserts that the argument is in there, but he isn't too surprised that some might find it hard to grasp. "What I'm trying to do is get people to see this point of view, that artificial intelligence and badly designed interfaces are equivalent," says Lanier. "It's very hard to get people to see who haven't seen that, but once it clicks into view, it's like an optical illusion, and they're amazed."

Maybe that's why, instead of describing himself as an A.I. critic, Lanier prefers to use the term "humanist." As Lanier will be the first to admit, it's a loaded term, evoking images of not only Cosimo de' Medici and Sir Isaac Newton but also the many scientists and philosophers whose theories he currently contests. At the same time, he notes, it's a convenient way to poke fun at the "post-human" imagery of most A.I.-themed books.

Asked how he came up with the term, Lanier's blue eyes roll upward and a playful smirk emerges. "Oh, I was just trying to be provocative," he says, swiping at another dreadlock. "I started using it at a conference in France just to upset them. I wanted to throw it in their face, how antihuman the notion of humanism has become."

Lanier's "them" is yet another attempt to put a defining banner over an amorphous opponent. Lanier can say this: In this case the opponent is a philosophical movement whose roots go back to two main sources: Richard Dawkins, an Oxford biologist and the author of the 1975 best-seller *The Selfish Gene,* and Daniel Dennett. Dawkins's "blind watchmaker" view of Darwinian evolution has encouraged modern technology designers to view evolution as a self-directed, optimizing process [www.world-of-dawkins.com/blind.htm].[2] Dennett's writings, meanwhile, have sought to minimize the traditional obstacles employed by philosophical critics of artificial intelligence, namely the argument that consciousness, a key pillar to intelligence, is a uniquely human phenomenon that can be defined only through subjective description. While Lanier does not dispute the ingenuity of either author, he does dispute the extremes to which their writings have been applied. He compares recent descriptions of technology as an extension of human evolution to other extreme examples of neo-Darwinist thought, such as *The Natural History of Rape*, by Randy Thornhill and Craig T. Palmer, a book which seeks to explain the phenomenon of rape through the context of evolution and natural selection. Such attempts, Lanier says, are merely examples of scientific inquiry, a field once devoted to stamping out superstition and dogmatic thinking, falling prey to its own dogmatic tendencies.

"I think we need to define a new type of humanism," he says. "I don't think I've done everything needed to create that definition, but I have to at least propose that we need one. That's because the reasons for needing it are different. What happened before was, we exaggerated one aspect of ourselves to the detriment of others in the world, and that was a mistake."

—

If Jaron Lanier's current definition of "humanism" seems ad hoc, Lanier has at least gone to the trouble of backing it up with a technological career devoted to improving the human experience. Born to an eclectic family—Lanier's mother was a classical pianist, his father a science writer—Lanier spent his childhood years playing music, studying science, and cultivating the kind of unique perspective that comes with living in a geodesic dome in the middle of rural New Mexico. Following his mother's death, Lanier dropped out of school and pursued a full-time career in classical music, only to drop back in a few years later when his passion for mathematics reasserted itself. Entering the University of New Mexico at the age of fifteen, Lanier studied mathematics until, like Hilbert a century before, he began to question his colleagues' overreliance on obfuscating symbols in representing universal ideas.

Describing the epiphany in a 1993 interview with *Wired,* Lanier said, "I decided that the way we present mathematics to each other is so obscure and bizarre that it makes something that's intrinsically beautiful and simple and appealing into something that's accessible only to people who have distorted personalities—like myself." [www.wired.com/wired/archive//1.02/jaron.html?person= jaron_lanier&topic_set=wiredpeople]

Lanier's solution: Build an interactive computer-graphics program that gives mathematicians the power to express their ideas in graphical form. To explore the idea further, Lanier learned to program computers. Disgusted by the arcane nature of most programming languages, Lanier soon applied his concept to the realm of software as well, developing the "visual" programming language that would eventually become the foundation for his first company, VPL, Inc. Lanier's software work eventually would lead to collaborations with Marvin Minsky, whom Lanier, like Kurzweil, still describes as an "important mentor" despite occasional disagreements.

While at VPL, Lanier developed a head-mounted device with embedded television monitors that put the user in the middle of a three-dimensional, computer-generated landscape. Dubbing this new style of interface "virtual reality," Lanier and his engineering colleagues became instant pioneers in one of the hottest technology fields of the late 1980s. Like their contemporaries in the commercial A.I. market, the VPL team attracted a horde of eager investors at first, only to watch those same investors run away as the projected VR market faltered. In 1992 one of the company's largest investors orchestrated a management coup, ousting Lanier as CEO and seizing Lanier's virtual-reality patents as collateral.[3]

Since the 1992 ouster, Lanier has bounced from project to project, mixing his affections for technology, art, and avant-garde music. Recent projects include the National Tele-Immersion Initiative and Internet 2, a potential high-bandwidth successor to today's text-driven Internet [www.advanced.org/teleimmersion.html]. Recent music projects include collaborations with the likes of Terry Riley, Will Calhoun [www.willcalhoun.com], and Sean Lennon [www.wired.com/news/culture/0,1284,38032,00.html]. Through it all, Lanier has become more firmly committed to a design philosophy that stresses computer technology as a medium for human expression. Hence his growing frustration with the so-called A.I. belief system, one that stresses machine autonomy and machine intelligence over human control. Lanier is not alone in this frustration. Past "user-friendly" interface advocates, most notably Doug Engelbart, the inventor of the computer mouse and the graphical-user interface, and Alan Kay, former Xerox PARC developer and godfather of the Apple Macintosh, waged their own historic battles against the A.I. camp, primarily over the issue of machine-oriented versus human-oriented design. Since the advent of the personal computer, however, such battles have faded into the background noise as developers struggle to keep up with the inexorable rate of hardware innovation.

"One thing that really breaks my heart is the loss of faith in the possibility for information tools to become much better than they are," says Lanier, shaking his head sadly. "Twenty years ago, people in the field would talk about designing an interface in which it would be natural for eight-year-olds to do what would now be considered advanced mathematics and physics. Could we design an interface so that people could have a far greater sharing of inner life than they do now? Could we design an interface that could give people a command of their memories that would transform and really open up life in a beautiful way? All those questions seem to have disappeared."

In their place stand a growing number of bug-ridden programs designed to exploit the latest advancements in microprocessor speed. Implicit within the modern programmer-user relationship is the belief that users will shoulder the design burden, either by putting up with shoddy software in exchange for access to the latest programs or by fixing the software themselves. While such a relationship is undoubtedly more market-oriented and market-driven, it also suggests a certain lack of effort on the original designer's part. Lanier derides the "psychology of abdication" that seems to permeate modern software development, viewing it as a betrayal both of the user and of machine capabilities.

Lanier does not put the blame for this psychology entirely on the shoulders of the A.I. research community, but he does see that community abetting its recent growth. By supporting the notion of computer intelligence as a stand-alone entity, A.I. researchers have made it easier for software programmers to build programs that ignore the intelligence of the human user.

Look into the current software marketplace, and it's easy to find examples of this trend. Clippie [http://www.businessweek.com/bwdaily/dnflash/jul2001/nf20010731_509.htm], the cartoon paperclip mascot in Microsoft Office programs, employs Bayesian belief networks, a form of artificial intelligence decision-making, to come up with the proper advice for frustrated Windows users. What some see as a helpful add-on, others have derided as intrusive, patronizing, or just plain annoying. From the Lanier perspective, Clippie and his software peers are merely a modern reworking of the Sorcerer's Apprentice. Look below the good intentions, and you'll find a lazy software designer using artificial intelligence to cover his tracks.

To get an idea as to where those tracks might lead, look no further than the performance of your average computer program, Lanier says. From the computer crash that devours an afternoon's worth of work to the "404 Page Unknown" error that pops up whenever an overtaxed server crumbles under traffic load, today's computer user has learned to factor in software failure as a central part of the everyday technology experience. Dubbing this state of affairs the "great shame" of the modern software industry, Lanier sees it as the number one argument against those who see the Moore's Law curve inevitably leading to thinking machines. "If you look at software, there's no Moore's Law going on; there's just stagnation," says Lanier.

Not only does Lanier dispute the Kurzweil view of humanlike machines by 2030, he offers an alternative view: a world in which every new computer program requires a permanent, on-call support person to help users navigate the endless array of bugs and poorly integrated features. "If Moore's Law is upheld for another 20 or 30 years, there will not only be a vast amount of computation going on planet Earth," writes Lanier, "but the maintenance of that computation will consume the efforts of almost every living person. We're talking a nation of help desks."

Such comments offer a sly poke at the extrapolation techniques used by Kurzweil and other modern authors. They also serve as a stepping-stone toward addressing the growing fascination with Darwinian theory in books and papers related to technology. For the record, Lanier does not denigrate the use of Darwin's evolutionary theories as an illustrative tool. What he does object to is the use of Darwin as a deus ex machina—a rescuing device designed to help lift engineers over current design barriers. "Cybernetic totalists are obsessed with Darwin," Lanier writes. "Darwin answers what would otherwise be a big hole in the Dogma: How will cybernetic systems be smart and creative enough to invent a post-human world?"

To offer a contrasting view of the future, Lanier cites Harvard professor Stephen Jay Gould, the author of *Full House: The Spread of Excellence from Plato to Darwin* and a vocal critic of Richard Dawkins. According to Gould, who once dismissed *Homo sapiens* as a "cosmic afterthought, a tiny little twig on the enormously arborescent bush of life," Darwinian evolution favors complexity over intelligence. Viewed from this perspective, tomorrow's computer systems will be even more chaotic, more bloated, and more problematic than today's already unwieldy systems.[4]

"I think what my main concern over Darwin comes down to is the willingness among some people to view things only from a quantitative perspective," says Lanier. "If you look at things from a qualitative perspective, we're nowhere. Qualitatively, we have a bunch of people using crappy old software that is embarrassing."

While such views might put him in a different category than the other, mostly philosophical critics of the A.I. camp, Lanier says he ultimately welcomes inclusion in the club. In addition to reinjecting a little healthy skepticism into the A.I. debate, Lanier sees himself as a valuable emissary. With his varied background—interface designer, musician, artist, author—Lanier is indeed adept at bridging the ideological chasm between the philosophers who have long railed against the A.I. field and the software developers simply trying to build better software programs. "What I'm trying to propose is that even to someone who's of a very hardheaded engineering mind, who doesn't go for all that soft humanities stuff, there are very pragmatic reasons to care about the philosophical viewpoint," says Lanier. "Without that aesthetic center, without that philosophical center, things fall apart very quickly."

Whether or not his fellow engineers take the message, Lanier doesn't particularly care. As a programmer and artist with eclectic tastes, Lanier is used to working in near obscurity. In fact, it might not be an exaggeration to say that he derives pleasure from it. Like the rock musician who sells only a thousand albums but spawns a thousand imitators in the process, Lanier seems willing to play the role of most frequently cited reference for future debate participants.

"I think I'm kind of an oddball," he says. "People are always telling me this, that I'm the only person inside the community who says these things or even cares about these things. I think I'm going to be less of an oddball over time, though. I've heard from young people who agree with me. I think as they take on positions of power there will be more of a school for humanistic computer science."

Chapter 5

—

THE PESSIMIST: BILL JOY

The phone rings. A woman tells me that Bill Joy is on the other end of the line, but before I'm patched through, she warns me that the Sun Microsystems chief scientist has less than twenty minutes to discuss his recent musings on the future of science and technology.

As soon as Joy gets on the phone, the estimate drops to fifteen minutes.

"We'll have to make this quick," he says, voice barely audible over the highway noise in the background. "My exit's coming up."

Twenty years ago, the idea of a software programmer dishing out hasty cellular-phone interviews à la Mick Jagger would have seemed absurd. Back then, the best way to find Joy or any other member of his social caste was to visit a college computer-science department or corporate headquarters and wind your way toward the deepest, darkest recesses of the building. There, wedged in between the stacks of paper and the air-conditioning ducts, you'd find a pasty-faced twenty-something male ready to tell you anything you wanted to know about software and computer systems, provided you: A) already knew how to program a computer and B) agreed to limit the interrogation to one question.

That was then. Today, the stereotypical troglodyte software programmer still flourishes in many corners of the world. For a growing number of elite programmers, however, programming has become a ticket to fame and fortune. For this new class of programmer, fielding calls from beseeching reporters and awestruck executives is as much a part of the job as writing software code. The subject of today's particular call is the April 2000 *Wired* magazine cover story. Penned by Joy in 1999, "Why the Future Doesn't Need Us" is a ten-thousand-word essay that pushes the programmer–as–rock star analogy even further [www.wirednews.com/wired/archive/8.04/joy.html]. Like George Harrison's Concert for Bangladesh in the 1970s and Bob Geldof's Live Aid in the 1980s, the essay is Joy's momentary attempt to reflect the glare created by the media spotlight onto an issue of increasing personal concern.

"I think it is no exaggeration to say we are on the cusp of the further perfection of extreme evil," writes Joy solemnly. "Accustomed to living with almost routine scientific breakthroughs, we have yet to come to terms with the fact that the most compelling 21st-century technologies—robotics, genetic engineering, and nanotechnology—pose a different threat than the technologies that have come before."

Since those words appeared in print, Joy has grown accustomed to reporters calling to flesh out their full meaning. Although not as admittedly incomplete as Jaron Lanier's "One-Half of a Manifesto," "Why the Future Doesn't Need Us" is still a rambling jazz riff open to subtly different interpretations. Joy credits a 1998 encounter with Ray Kurzweil for motivating the work. Given this genesis, is "Why the Future Doesn't Need Us" yet another indictment of A.I. advocates' hubris? Joy, for one, doesn't see it that way.

"I want to be careful to say that I don't share as much concern about A.I. as other people have," he says. "The areas I'm most concerned with in the near term are biotech and robotics. Any concern with [artificial] life and artificial intelligence is much further out."

That's not to say that Joy dismisses the issue of artificial intelligence altogether. One of the main threads holding "Why the Future Doesn't Need Us" together is Joy's equivocal stance on the issue of machine autonomy. A skeptic by training, Joy says it was that initial encounter with Kurzweil that forced him to ask the dreaded "What if?" question. As in: What if thinking machines really are possible, given current exponential growth rates? As a man intimately familiar with software programs and their capacity for mutation and evolution, Joy says he found the question troubling to say the least.

"Everybody sees the world through the perspective of their own personal histories, I suppose," he says. "I'm certain my background had something to do with the way 'Why the Future Doesn't Need Us' came out. I think I've seen how difficult it is to build things that are reliable, certainly engineered systems. It's a humbling thing. Even though some of my programs have been a success, I've realized how difficult and unlikely it was."

The result, admits Joy, is a viewpoint that arms both sides of the modern A.I. debate. Like Lanier, Joy sees little within the current state of computer-software development to suggest the emergence of sentient machines. "Despite some progress, the problems that remain are even more daunting," he writes. Like Kurzweil, however, Joy has learned to respect software technology's capacity for surprise. "It's kind of like the old saying 'There's a first time for everything,'" says Joy. "In this case, since we're creating the tools that can create these first times, I think, we can't dismiss them out of hand. Extraordinary events only have to happen once, and the fundamental definition of extraordinary events is that they can't be predicted by past events."

The end result is a position that leans toward the credulity of Kurzweil and Moravec but balances it with a deeper sense of foreboding. It is a position Joy best summarizes when factoring in his own experiences as a technology designer. "Having struggled my entire career to build reliable software systems," he writes, "it seems to me more than likely that this future will not work out as well as some people may imagine. My personal experience suggests we tend to overestimate our design abilities."

—

Bill Joy's journey from boiler-room hacker to quotable pundit is itself a reflection of the growing power and complexity of software. A gifted mathematics student, Joy fell in love with computers during his undergraduate years at the University of Michigan. Like Hilbert and Turing before him, Joy found the building of rigidly formal systems that could break the universe down into true and untrue statements intensely "seductive." Lured by the siren song emanating from the local campus computer lab, Joy soon began to delve deeper and deeper into the art of computer programming.

For his graduate work, Joy headed out to the University of California at Berkeley. This was in 1975, the same year that AT&T scientist and UNIX creator Ken Thompson, a Berkeley alumnus, began a one-year sabbatical at his alma mater. The Berkeley computer-science department had just pooled all its money to purchase a new mainframe computer, the DEC 11/70, and Thompson and a few other department staff members were in the process of writing a new version of UNIX to serve as the machine's operating system. Intrigued by the prospect of working on what, at the time, qualified as a supercomputing system, Joy quickly joined in the effort, writing a program in the tutorial language Pascal. When Thompson ended his visit to Berkeley, Joy and fellow grad student Chuck Haley took over the UNIX rewriting project, creating an entirely new version, dubbed the "Berkeley Software Distribution," or BSD.[1]

Looking back in his *Wired* essay, Joy describes BSD as the classic example of a software industry "success failure," a program that becomes so popular that it soon takes over the life of its original creator. In an effort to speed development, Joy offered free copies of the BSD source code—the line-by-line instructions that dictated what the computer did and when it would do it—to programmers at other universities and research laboratories. Soon Joy was receiving a steady stream of bug reports and suggestions for new features. By mid-1978, the number of people requesting copies, asking questions, and soliciting advice had grown so much that Joy was spending less time pursuing his studies and more time mailing tapes and answering the phone.

BSD's popularity in the academic world would have major long-term effects, both on Joy's career and on the future of the computer industry. A key part of BSD's popularity was that the program's liberal license allowed users to modify it for use on machines besides the DEC 11/70 without first asking for permission. As BSD appeared on more machines, developers of the ARPAnet, an academic precursor of the Internet, began treating BSD as the default operating system for the growing assortment of Internet protocols. By the early 1980s, businesses were starting to catch on to the advantages of a zero-cost, freely modifiable software operating system as well.

One such company was a start-up out of Palo Alto, California, calling itself Sun Microsystems. In 1982, after six years of devoting more and more time to BSD, Joy decided to forgo the Ph.D. route and join the Sun staff. While at Sun, Joy built his reputation as a master craftsman even further, serving as chief designer for the company's new line of workstations—low-cost, BSD-driven computers designed to provide an alternative to traditional mainframe systems such as the DEC 11 series. Like BSD, the workstations' popularity provided yet another hint of the shifting power dynamics within corporate culture. Programmers who'd once yielded to the dictates of upper management when it came to computer-system procurement were now demanding workstations because it meant continued access to BSD, ARPAnet, and other perks unavailable to programmers in the mainframe computing world.

By 1990, Joy's clout within Sun Microsystems had grown to the point where he requested and received his own personal laboratory in the Colorado mountains. There, Joy and a select team of Sun engineers worked on a number of cutting-edge projects, including Java, a streamlined programming language first developed by James Gosling, and Jini, a set of Java-based tools designed to give all devices, from mainframe computers to ordinary household appliances, the ability to communicate and share information over the Internet. Like an architect working on the Tower of Babel, Joy's last two decades have been devoted to reining in the forces he helped unleash back in the 1970s. In a 1999 speech to fellow software developers, Joy described his career as a prolonged effort in "managing complexity" in both hardware and software systems.[2] "There's an enormous advantage to keeping the design simple and clean," Joy says.

It hasn't been an easy job. In the course of watching his personal creations grow and propagate according to invisible market forces, Joy has become increasingly receptive to the Kurzweil view that tomorrow's programs will evolve in a manner similar to today's living organisms. "I think evolution is the strongest tool that we have for providing [intelligent] behavior, and if you can create an artificial context in which you can create a population or an ecology which then through evolution adapts, you can cause various interesting things to emerge," he says.

Joy cites examples such as Kumar Chellapilla and David B. Fogel's checkers program [www.cs.buffalo.edu/~rapaport/572/S01/checkers.html]. Chellapilla, a UC San Diego graduate student, and Fogel, a computer scientist with the San Diego–based company Natural Selection, Inc., developed a neural-network-based program with the ability to improve itself through self-play. After plugging in only the basic rules, Chellapilla and Fogel watched as the program stumbled at first but improved with each passing game. By using genetic algorithms to weed out the weakest moves and board positions, the program managed to improve its performance to expert level without human input.

Building a program that outcompetes humans in the narrow arena of checkers is a long way removed from building a program that outcompetes humans in the arena of natural translation. In fact, it is a skill A.I. researchers have mastered since Arthur Samuel unveiled the first championship-level checkers program in the early 1960s. Still, the success of the genetic algorithm method leads Joy to believe that tomorrow's software programs will have a much better ability to assist in their own development. "I think calling the programming of a robot or an artificial consciousness, say, fifty years from now 'software' is to confuse ourselves," he says. "It's not going to be done in a way where someone's sitting in front of a screen and cutting and pasting with a text editor. It's not really software in the terms that we currently understand."

Unlike Kurzweil, however, Joy sees this drift toward machine autonomy as a cause for concern. As he notes in "Why the Future Doesn't Need Us," a program doesn't have to be intelligent to be a problem. Witness the growing number of computer viruses, e-mail "worms," and "Trojan horses." Written by malicious pranksters or unwitting programmers, these contagionlike programs contain little or no intelligence yet still have the ability to self-replicate, sending copies out over the Internet to attack or infect other machines. Although they are relatively harmless from a human-safety perspective, Joy says it isn't hard to envision a more grave scenario when the power of self-replication is extended to bioengineered plants and self-evolving machines.

"Actually we're already seeing lots of examples of this in the genetic-foods area," Joy says. "You've got the example of StarLink corn, the genetically modifed corn that wasn't supposed to get into the human food supply but did. You've got diseases jumping from one species to another via contaminated livestock feed. This is just the tip of the iceberg." [www.purefood.org/ge/starlink300.cfm]

The issue of self-replicating robots may seem a little far-fetched today, but Joy is confident that the means for this type of technology will become available within the current decade. Joy lists his growing fascination with the science of nanotechnology as another reason for writing the *Wired* essay. An umbrella term used to encompass engineering techniques at the molecular or "nanometer" scale (one nanometer equals one-billionth of a meter), nanotechnology has emerged from the pages of science fiction over the last decade. Researchers at IBM and Yale University have already demonstrated the ability to position individual atoms, building molecular-sized circuits and switching devices. Already the speculation is rampant over how to employ this technology in the construction of future computer systems.[3]

Another logical step, as Joy is quick to point out, is the development of "universal constructors," molecular devices that can fabricate copies of themselves. Once such a device is created, molecular engineers will be able to employ the same binary logic and self-referencing, or "recursive," design techniques used by software engineers. Instead of an endless stream of ones and zeros, however, the base units of this construction process will be millions of tiny machines working in parallel.

While such a scenario seems ideal—imagine building a device atom by atom with little or no wasted by-products—it also opens up a whole new range of risky possibilities. Unlike software programs, the results of a runaway nanotechnology algorithm would do more than just eat up computer memory. They could devour resources and raw materials necessary to living organisms. In one nightmare sequence, which Joy and nanotech experts whimsically dub the "gray goo" problem, the devices keep constructing new copies, much like fast-dividing cancer cells, until the entire surface of the planet is covered with the same bloblike artificial substance.[4]

Admittedly, such outcomes have little to do with the traditional risks associated with artificial intelligence. Still, they provide a colorful alternative to the Hollywood-driven image of humanoid robots. As a technologist who has spent his career managing complexity, Joy expresses more concern over "gray goo" and other unintended outcomes than over malevolent machines. Contrasting his "gray goo" scenario with Kurzweil's "spiritual machines," Joy says both outcomes are possible but only the first one takes into account the recent history of technological evolution. "Ray [Kurzweil] clearly is interested in uploading consciousness into a silicon brain, so he's looking at the amount of computing power it takes to make that possible," says Joy. "My point of view is that a robot doesn't have to be conscious to be dangerous. A robot species that's wild is dangerous, because once it's a species, once it can evolve, we really can't predict what it's going to do."

Kurzweil, however, doesn't see much of a difference between his outlook and Joy's. "Bill and I have been frequently paired in a variety of venues as pessimist and optimist respectively," writes Kurzweil in the on-line précis for his upcoming book, *The Singularity Is Near.* "Although I'm expected to criticize Bill's position, and indeed I do take issue with his prescription of relinquishment, I nonetheless usually end up defending Joy on the key issue of feasibility. Recently a Nobel Prize–winning panelist dismissed Bill's concerns, exclaiming that 'we're not going to see self-replicating nanoengineered entities for a hundred years.' I pointed out that one hundred years was indeed a reasonable estimate of the amount of technical progress required to achieve this particular milestone *at today's rate of progress.* But because we're doubling the rate of progress every decade, we'll see a century of progress—*at today's rate*—in only twenty-five calendar years" [www.kurzweilai.net/articles/art0134.html?printable="].

Joy, too, disagrees with those who would conveniently categorize him as a pessimist. "If I wasn't optimistic about these technologies, if I didn't believe that capitalism would drive them forward, then I wouldn't be concerned," he writes.

Nevertheless, the "prescription of relinquishment," to which Kurzweil alludes, has been a cause for consternation within some corners of the A.I. research community. In "Why the Future Doesn't Needs Us" Joy says his biggest concern in regard to self-replicating machines has less to do with the machines' intentions than with human intentions. In a world already brimming with risks, the capacity of a single designer to wreak havoc, either unintentionally or intentionally, is automatically heightened when technology has the power to self-replicate. Before unleashing this kind of power, scientists and engineers should first ask whether this type of power is desirable.

Not surprisingly, many A.I. researchers whose projects currently show little capacity for self-replication, much less full-scale autonomy, have questioned Joy's tone. "I found it slightly disingenuous for Joy to announce that robotics is the next big threat to mankind, when most people working in robotics and A.I. are barely scratching out a living," writes Richard Wallace, a developer with the ALICE on-line chatterbot project. "We would all like to found successful companies like Sun and become wealthy philosophers. But the last thing we need right now is more government regulations or the kind of negative publicity that gives pause to our investors. Our small start-ups are hardly as threatening as nuclear proliferation." [www.wired.com/wired/archive/8.07/rants_pr.html]

From Joy's perspective, the threat posed by artificial intelligence has less to do with destructive power than with the heightened capacity for individual mischief. In the case of nuclear proliferation, central governments have done a fairly good job over the last half century of keeping nuclear devices out of the hands of ordinary citizens and partisan groups. In the case of self-replicating robots, a single individual running a software program downloaded off the Internet could set off a chain reaction with potentially grievous consequences.

Again, Joy's concerns reflect a career working in the software trenches. Over the last two decades, software companies have painfully learned to accept the consequences of doing business over the Internet—loss of centralized software control, increased piracy, and unrestricted copying—in exchange for higher profits and the streamlined delivery channels afforded by Internet distribution. As other fields of technology come to resemble software development in terms of design and distribution, these fields, too, will have to learn to accommodate heightened security risks. In other words, Joy says, imagine a nanotechnology equivalent of a fax machine, a device in every home that manufactures items of personal necessity simply by downloading the molecular plans off the Internet. Now imagine the nanotechnology equivalent of an e-mail virus or a mail bomb, a malicious program that seizes control of that machine, making it pump out noxious fumes instead of useful products.

"Information is hard to control, and you now have powerful tools to manipulate it," intones Joy. "If everything is information, then everything dangerous is information. Hence the problem, because all the traditional mechanisms we've had in society for controlling access to dangerous stuff break down in the natural way that information breaks down control."

Such comments draw an immediate critique from Kurzweil, who believes that the ability to assimilate and adapt to new technology is an inherent trait of human culture. "I do take some comfort in the way we have dealt with software viruses," Kurzweil says. "It's a new form of pathogen. It didn't exist before. And it continues to be a concern, but we've been able to relegate it to a relative nuisance. The combination of ethical standards, technological safeguards, and, occasionally, law enforcement have been able to keep that from becoming an enormous danger. Now, somebody might say, 'Wait a minute, software viruses don't generally kill people,' but that only strengthens my argument, because when we have self-replicating technology that is potentially lethal, the ethical standards, the efforts to put in technological safeguards, the law enforcement responses are going to be one hundred times greater."

Joy, for his part, isn't so sure. Unless scientists are willing to re-evaluate the fundamental tenets of their culture—tenets that ensure open access to scientific data, even if that means letting the data fall into the hands of nefarious individuals—he sees cause for concern. Near the end of "Why the Future Doesn't Need Us," Joy sums up this concern with a pessimistic shrug. "I have always believed that making software more reliable, given its many uses, will make the world a safer and better place," he writes. "If I were to come to believe the opposite, then I would be morally obligated to stop this work. I can now imagine such a day may come."

Since he wrote those words, Joy's critics, including Kurzweil, have interpreted this stance as a passive endorsement for government regulation and "totalitarian" restriction. "You can't separate out the good technology from the bad," Kurzweil says. "The same technology that can cure cancer or provide powerful new treatments can also be used by a terrorist to create a bioengineered pathogen. It's just two different uses of the same power."

Joy, on the other hand, says controlling information isn't the goal. The goal, he says, is to force scientists to recognize the heightened risk associated with modern research. The scientific community can address those risks in a number of ways. It can force members to take the equivalent of a Hippocratic oath, using peer pressure and a self-imposed system of ethics to regulate research and technology design. It can turn to the insurance industry and let market forces dictate the level of allowable risk. Or it can turn to the government.

"We'll never get the risk to be zero," Joy admits, "but I am interested in seeing us reduce it in a sensible way. Life without risk is not life, just like life without death isn't life. Isn't that what we learn at the beginning of every vampire movie? I think it's the same thing with technology and the future."

The fifteen minutes allotted for our phone conversation have turned into twenty-five, and the highway noise in the background has long since given way to birds chirping as Joy grants me one final question. Seizing this comment, I decide to bring up the notion of fear, both in its traditional guise—machines usurping the power of humanity—and in its more modern disguises. Scratch the surface of the current obsession with "spiritual machines" and self-replicating robots and it's hard not to detect a certain similarity to the fears and hopes expressed in the recent Y2K hysteria. One man's cataclysm is another man's rapture, after all. Given the timing of recent works such as "Why the Future Doesn't Need Us," isn't it possible that technologists are simply voicing their own concerns?

Joy weighs the question momentarily. "Do you mean a premillennial-angst sort of thing?" he asks.

When I answer yes, Joy pauses again before answering. "I think the timing is coincidental. I think the human genome project, computers becoming powerful, biology becoming an information science, these are contemporary events. They're not related to whether the year ends in zero zero."

That's not to say the arrival of a new century doesn't provide special opportunities. After noting in "Why the Future Doesn't Need Us" that humanity is "being propelled into this new century with no plan, no control, no brakes," Joy says that the arrival of a fresh century is a bit like the arrival of a new year. It offers a chance to make new resolutions, set new goals, and put a check on the unhealthy behaviors of the past.

"When you want to talk about the future, you can't of course predict anything exactly, but you can look at what you think are the range of possible futures," Joy says. "So, for example, if you're a hundred pounds overweight, I can tell you how it will affect your life expectancy. I won't be able to tell you how long you're going to live, but it changes the distribution and the likely average and different nature of the outcomes. In the same way, if you're playing with these dangerous things in careless ways, it clearly changes the distribution of possible or likely outcomes. We don't have to agree on even what the ranges are to come to an agreement that maybe some behavior modification is necessary. I think each of us, with our individual perception, can see that adoption of more sanity is in our interest, even if we don't agree exactly how much."

Chapter 6

—

FACT VERSUS FICTION

It was supposed to be a joke, a bunch of scientists and science-fiction fans paying homage to a favorite movie character, but when Stanford professor David Stork decided to put together a mock birthday celebration for HAL, the fictional computer antagonist in the movie *2001: A Space Odyssey,* little did he know how seriously some people would take it.

"A lot of Silicon Valley types showed up," Stork says, remembering the event. "[A.I. researcher] Donald Knuth came over. Daniel Dennett wanted to come but couldn't make it because of scheduling issues. He's very well connected with the media, though. He told somebody at the Associated Press, and they sent over a cameraman. The next thing I knew, it had turned into a full-blown media event."

Looking back, Stork isn't too surprised that so many people would turn out to commemorate a malevolent computer character. In the world of software engineering, where struggling with insubordinate machines is part of the job description, most programmers can quote verbatim passages of HAL's dialogue from the 1968 movie, including the famous death scene, during which HAL reveals that he first became "operational" at the University of Illinois on January 12, 1992. Stork can't help but chuckle whenever he recalls the photo that appeared the following day in newspapers around the globe. The picture depicts Stork cutting into a cake with the words "Happy Birthday HAL" emblazoned on it. A plastic replica of the red light used to represent HAL's "eye" in the movie sits atop the cake. For further comedic effect, Stork says, he had the light rigged up to an electric circuit so that a nearby friend could slowly lower the voltage while he and other partygoers sang a rendition of "Daisy." "A friend sent me a copy of the photo from Thailand," Stork says [http://rii.ricoh.com/~stork/].

If the media's eagerness took Stork by surprise, it also planted the seeds of a project that would blossom a half decade later. Thanks to a minor discrepancy between the book version of *2001* and the film, Stork knew that he and fellow *2001* fans would get a second chance to conduct their birthday celebration in 1997. According to movie legend, director Stanley Kubrick changed HAL's birthday from the 1997 date listed in the screenplay—cowritten with Kubrick by book author Arthur C. Clarke—in the belief that audience members might feel more empathy for an older computer during the movie's termination scene. Although less faithful to the movie, a January 12, 1997, celebration fell closer to the thirtieth anniversary of the movie's release and the movie's title date. With five years to prepare, Stork began assembling *HAL's Legacy: 2001's Computer as Dream and Reality,* a book exploring the links and gulfs between the movie's fictional representation of artificial intelligence and the modern study of A.I.

"Every once in a while you have to look back," says Stork, who now divides his time between working on the Stanford faculty and serving as chief scientist for Ricoh Silicon Valley. He contrasts *HAL's Legacy* with the growing number of A.I. books seeking to reassert the speculative efforts of Clarke and Kubrick. "The A.I. field has always been a magnet for extravagant claims and bold predictions. By looking back, you keep people honest," he says.

In the process of looking back, Stork, who admits to having seen the film forty-three times, says his respect for *2001* has only increased. In an attempt to fulfill Kubrick's stated ambition of making "a really good sci-fi movie," the screenplay's co-authors interviewed an army of aerospace engineers, astronauts, and computer scientists.[1] The result, at least in the movie's dominant middle act, is one of the most realistic depictions of space travel outside of a documentary film. "Kubrick and Clarke took a lot of effort to get the science right," Stork says. "It's one of the things that distinguishes *2001* from other science-fiction films, and it's one of the major reasons, I believe, *2001* remains so popular within the scientific community."

In the case of artificial intelligence, however, the continuing resonance of the *2001* story line and the HAL character goes beyond simple admiration of the authors' zest for future vérité. As its title suggests, *HAL's Legacy* is no mere fan book. It explores the science of *2001* from a modern perspective, incorporating the insight of scientists currently working to fill in the technical gaps Kubrick and Clarke expected to be filled in by now. Included among its chapters is a review of HAL's approach to common sense written by Cyc project leader Doug Lenat, a review of HAL's ability to recognize and understand human speech by voice-interface expert Raymond Kurzweil, and a general chapter on the basic hardware needs of a computer with HAL-like capabilities, titled "Could We Build HAL?" written by David Kuck, a former director of the Center for Supercomputing Research and Development at the University of Illinois.

According to Stork, the answer to Kuck's question is yes, but with an immediate asterisk. "There are supercomputers today with roughly the power we'd expect in a HAL-type system," Stork says. "The problem is we just don't know how to program those computers to perform the A.I. tasks we wish."

In the thirty-plus years since the release of *2001,* that asterisk, like the unblinking red eye of HAL himself, has taunted A.I. researchers. What seemed to be so realistic and believable by the turn of the century now seems realistic and believable only when you extend the prediction timeline out to 2020 or 2030. Not surprisingly, many within the A.I. community—and many outside of it—wonder if the whole pursuit of HAL-like machines isn't just a treadmill exercise masquerading as scientific research. In explaining the purpose of his book, Stork himself sees the growing discrepancy between expectation and reality as demanding a re-evaluation of HAL's archetypal role.

"As we approach 2001, we might ask why we have not matched the dream of making a HAL," writes Stork in the book's opening chapter. "The reasons are instructive. In a broad overview, we have met, and surpassed, the vision of HAL in those domains—speech, hardware, planning, chess—that can be narrowly defined and easily specified. But in domains such as language understanding and common sense, which are basically limitless in their possibilities and hard to specify, we fall far short. Perhaps too we need to ask whether, as a culture, we are willing to support the undertaking of producing artificial intelligence."

If trying to live up to the HAL mythos seems frustrating, Stork recognizes that A.I. researchers have only themselves and their predecessors to blame. Because of Kubrick and Clarke's due diligence in soliciting input from top scientists in the field—Kubrick at one point employed A.I. MIT lab director Marvin Minsky as a consultant—*2001* stands as a veritable time capsule of the optimistic attitudes and predictions that characterized the A.I. research culture during the 1960s. Indeed, given the A.I. community's long history of ego battles and academic infighting, the HAL archetype offers one of the few attempts to forge a community consensus outside of the original 1956 and 1957 Dartmouth summer conferences. "Looking back at the 1960s, I think it's amazing that Kubrick and Clarke made a coherent vision at all," Stork says. "I think there were only two or three computer-science departments in the country at the time."

Add it all up, and you have a vision that still manages to resonate within the hearts and minds of modern A.I. researchers. Even though technology has in many areas veered away from the extrapolated course plotted out by Kubrick and Clarke, both HAL and the surrounding *2001* story line provide a totemic link to the glory days of A.I. research. For modern A.I. researchers, the power of that link is hard to overestimate.

"Every culture has some central, pervasive story," says James Hendler, professor of computer science at the University of Maryland. "Some people say you can't fully understand Japanese culture without understanding the story of the forty-seven ronin. I think it's the same with *2001* and the A.I. community."

Not everyone within the A.I. community is comfortable with this link. Pat Hayes, a scientist at the Institute for Human Machine Cognition in Pensacola, Florida, sees HAL as less of an archetype and more akin to the Ancient Mariner's albatross—that is, a permanent reminder of the A.I. community's ill-conceived early intentions. Instead of blaming Kubrick and Clarke, however, Hayes traces those ill-conceived intentions directly back to Turing, who put forward the notion that the best application of artificial intelligence is a computer capable of imitating human thought and behavior. "If you look at the work that gets done and gets reported at A.I. conferences, nobody is working toward the imitation of human beings," says Hayes. "Most modern A.I. work is aimed toward making the machine smarter and more useful to the human user. And yet this notion of building artificial humans is the image most people still have of A.I."

Current trends in commercial A.I. applications support Hayes's viewpoint. Where technologists have avoided the prospect of building a mirrorlike intelligence in favor of technologies that seek to augment some facet of the user's own intelligence, the results have registered immediate impact. Take, for example, the Google search engine. One of the Web's most popular search tools, Google employs an autonomous program that works with many of the same heuristic search algorithms employed by the earliest A.I. programs. Although fairly mundane from a Turing perspective, Google's usability has made it a valuable reference tool for researchers trying to rein in the complexity of the Internet. "I couldn't live without it," laughs Hayes. "It's come to the point where I throw a keyword in Google, and it gets the example I need faster than if I walked across the room and picked the book up off the shelf."

The result, Hayes says, is a program that better fits not only the technology—in this case the ever-expanding Internet—but also the reason humans turn to technology in the first place. In an effort to break the A.I. community's obsession with Turing-style machines, both he and Ken Ford, director of the Institute for Human Machine Cognition, wrote an article for a 1998 *Scientific American* special issue on intelligence. Titled "On Computational Wings: Rethinking the Goals of Artificial Intelligence," the article likens the current HAL-inspired reappraisal of artificial intelligence to the invention of the first heavier-than-air aircraft at the beginning of the twentieth century.

Just as today's researchers work in the shadow of HAL, Hayes says, aviation pioneers like the Wright brothers had to find ways to break free of the pseudoscientific assumptions of their predecessors. "For millennia, flying was one of humanity's fondest dreams," the authors write. "The prehistory of aeronautics, both popular and scholarly, dwelled on the idea of imitating bird flight, usually by somehow attaching flapping wings to a human body or to a framework worked by a single person."

By 1900, the Wright brothers and their European counterparts had moved away from the flapping-wing model of flight. And yet even when their experiments showed signs of success, more than a few scientific onlookers dismissed the fixed-wing approach as not true flight. "Aerial flight is one of the great class of problems with which man can never cope," wrote American Astronomical Society president Simon Newcomb in a memoir published in 1903. "The construction of an aerial vehicle which could carry even a single man from place to place at pleasure, requires the discovery of some new metal or some new force."

The moral of the story, say Ford and Hayes, is that instead of treating intelligent machines as a looking glass to explore our own quirks and inconsistencies, scientists should dispense with the Turing model altogether and build machines that leverage existing human intelligence. Dubbing this approach the "cognitive prosthesis" model of A.I., the authors say the results could be just as revolutionary as the Wright brothers' decision to stop building birds and start building planes. "Our intelligent machines already surpass us in many ways," Hayes and Ford write. "The most useful computer applications, including A.I. applications, are valuable exactly by virtue of their lack of humanity. A truly humanlike program would be just as useless as a truly pigeonlike aircraft."

Such eagerness to scrap the vision of HAL-like computers grates on the ears of A.I. pioneers who helped contribute to that vision. In an interview in the second chapter of *HAL's Legacy,* Marvin Minsky, now working with the MIT media lab, laughs off the argument that HAL is an unreachable ideal. Later in the interview, Stork notes that today's computer designers have yet to develop a program capable of both playing chess and conversing with human beings the way HAL does in one famous scene. Minsky's response is emphatic: "But we could have! Only a small community has concentrated on general intelligence. No one has tried to make a thinking machine and then teach it chess."

Far from seeing HAL as an archetype, Minsky sees HAL as an example of what could have been if researchers had only been willing to keep their eyes on the proper target. Instead of advancing en masse on the objective of general intelligence, the A.I. research community divided its forces in the years immediately following the release of *2001.* Although smaller targets such as pattern recognition, machine-based learning, and computer chess have fallen, "the true majesty of general intelligence still awaits our attack."

In an April 2001 speech at the fifteenth annual Game Developers Conference in San Jose, California, Minsky once again addressed the A.I. community's failure to deliver HAL-like machines. This time around, however, the A.I. pioneer expressed hope that the tangled threads of A.I. research might be rewoven into a single coherent theory [http://technetcast.ddj.com/tnc_play_stream.html? stream_id=526]. "The human brain is a wonderful kludge that has built lots of different kinds of control systems. You shift from one to another, but some of your common sense says what you can shift to," said Minsky. "People are always arguing, should I use a relational database? Should I represent it in the neural net? Should I represent it as a fuzzy-logic set? Should I represent it as a bunch of axioms in mathematical logic? The answer to all of those is no. You should use all of them."

In other words, in their attempts to mimic human thought and human behavior, human researchers should be willing to get as down and dirty as nature has in manufacturing the human mind. For this reason, HAL and the other sentient machines depicted in science fiction remain a valuable asset to A.I. research. Not only do they provide a polestar to keep the study of machine intelligence on track, they also provide a challenge to system designers.

The University of Maryland's James Hendler agrees. "If you look at the history of artificial intelligence, the best breakthroughs have always come as a response to some challenge," he says. "The theory of computation didn't become reality until the early researchers realized they needed machines to crack codes during World War II. The math for chess programs didn't get developed until Simon, Shannon, and others embraced the challenge of teaching a computer how to play chess. At the very least, HAL provides a common target."

Besides, Hendler says, it also provides a valuable reference point for the world outside of A.I. research. "When I tell nontechnical people I'm working on artificial intelligence, they sometimes get that blank look in their eyes," says Hendler. "When I tell them I'm trying to create Lieutenant Commander Data [from *Star Trek*], suddenly their eyes light up."

Relying on science fiction as a way to communicate goals to the general population is a risky venture at best. Not all movie directors are as vigilant as Kubrick in presenting the future of science. Most have preferred to expand upon the darker themes traditionally associated with A.I. Indeed, judging by such recent movies as *The Matrix* and *Terminator 2,* intelligent machines have become the ideal Hollywood bad guy of the post–Cold War world: emotionless, hard-to-kill entities with no political lobby to protest stereotypical on-screen characterizations.

In literature the evolution of artificial intelligence as a storytelling device seems closer to the evolution of the artificial-intelligence debate. Whereas past authors such as Isaac Asimov and Philip K. Dick explored the barriers to and implications of machines passing for human beings, today's authors seem more concerned with the inevitability of this idea. In books such as *Exegesis,* written by Carnegie Mellon researcher Astro Teller [www.cs.cmu.edu/~astro/], and *Galatea 2.2,* written by Richard Powers [http://eserver.org/clogic/2-2/williams.html], the story narrator is a researcher who comes to the lab one morning to find that his or her A.I. project has undergone a Pinocchio-like transformation during the night. In each instance the author focuses more on how the protagonist handles the sudden onset of responsibility—not to mention the sudden recognition of personal ignorance—than on the behavior of the machine itself.

In *Galatea 2.2,* the protagonist, also named Richard Powers, sums up the internal angst when he comes across his program, named Helen, singing a verse he himself had been singing in the laboratory only a few days before.

She was stuck on the first phrase, that unfinished half-stitch, because that's all I'd sung to her. Becauses that's where I had stuck. After twenty-five years, I could not remember how the rest of the tune went. Over and back Helen hummed, not knowing she possessed but half the melodic story. Bounce me up to Jericho. Lack of tonal resolution did not faze her. No one told her that tunes were supposed to come home to tonic. This was the only one anybody had ever sung her.

And in that moment, I understood that I, too, would never have a handle on metaphor. For here was the universe in a grain of literal sand. Singing—enabled, simulated on a silicon substrate. I felt how a father must feel, seeing his unconscious gestures—pushing back a forelock or nudging the sink cabinet shut with a toe—picked up and mimicked by a tiny son.[2]

Such a passage intertwines all three of the major threads in the current A.I. debate. From Kurzweil's notion of artificial intelligence as manifest destiny to Lanier's notion of A.I. as humanistic inquiry taken to its ridiculous extremes to Joy's notion of A.I. as yet another stepping-stone to greater existential uncertainty, Powers examines the here-and-now possibility of a machine with Turing-level skills and asks the troubling question it inspires: *Now what?* Gone, if only for a moment, are the usual science-fiction concerns: machines masquerading as humans, machines overthrowing their masters, and machines failing to comprehend uniquely human notions such as love, hate, tragedy, and comedy.

If this trend seems cutting edge, true students of the genre know better. In addressing the role of the creator, recent authors have brought the HAL mythos full circle, connecting it once again with the fictional story lines that have framed the A.I. debate from the beginning: Mary Shelley's *Frankenstein,* the golem of Hebrew folklore, and the Greek myth of Pygmalion, the Cypriot sculptor whose favorite statue, Galatea, magically comes to life. The title of Powers's book, *Galatea 2.2,* underlines the homage.

When it comes to bringing the HAL mythos full circle, however, perhaps the most overt example is the 2001 film *A.I.* Written by Kubrick and directed by Steven Spielberg following Kubrick's death in 1998, *A.I.* re-examines the human-machine tension of *2001*'s second act in the light of modern attitudes. In *2001* Kubrick introduces the irony of a machine acting more human than the human characters surrounding it. In *A.I.* Spielberg revives this irony while, at the same time, pointing out the instinctual resentment humans feel toward anything that dares to appear more "intelligent" or human than they are.

Compared with books like *Exegesis* and *Galatea 2.2,* Spielberg's vision is hard to place within the current A.I. landscape. On the one hand, its humanoid characters seem like a jump back to the "golden age" of A.I.—not to mention the golden age of science fiction. On the other hand, *A.I.* offers its own celluloid time capsule to the future. It puts a lid on what Bill Joy might call "the premillennial-angst sort of thing." It even endorses, albeit in a highly indirect manner, the Kurzweil attack on the "great man" theory of artificial intelligence by presenting humanity as more obstacle than aid in the overall process of machine evolution.

Stork, for one, hesitates to evaluate *A.I.* in the same light as *2001*. Although Kubrick played a major role in the making of both films, Stork sees the current fictional interest in artificial intelligence as less a reflection of popular attitudes and more a reflection of Hollywood's current eagerness to put storytelling ahead of true science. "There is one important lesson that comes out of *A.I.*," he says. "*2001* said artificial intelligence would be based on the mainframe computer model. *A.I.* says no, it's robotics. This is a major strand in current philosophy. People like [MIT researcher] Rodney Brooks and the other robot people say we need to build things that interact with the world. I think that philosophy has a lot to commend itself, but I also think that the real action in artificial intelligence is going to be in other places, most notably the Internet."

To back up that belief, Stork has launched the Open Mind Initiative, a project that attempts to tap the rapidly expanding population of Internet users [www.OpenMind.org/index.shtml]. Like the Cyc project, Open Mind aims to collect snippets of commonsense wisdom and compile them into a universal knowledge base. Unlike Cyc, however, Open Mind has pledged to make the resulting knowledge base and software tools that derive from it "open source"—that is, freely available to any user who wants to inspect or download the software source code [www.opensource.org/docs/definition.html]. Taking inspiration from popular free software projects such as GNU Emacs [www.gnu.org/software/emacs/emacs.es.html] and Linux, Stork says his intention is to include as many participants as possible. "We need to harvest the knowledge of large groups of people," Stork says. "In looking at open-source projects I noticed two important trends: The number of collaborators per project has increased over time. Emacs in the 1970s had roughly one hundred. Linux has up to ten thousand contributors. I'm projecting that in the future we could have up to 100 million collaborators on some projects."

Stork sees another trend: As the number of collaborators goes up, the average level of expertise per participant has decreased. "The people who did free software twenty years ago were real hackers," he says. "Now anybody can contribute. All we have to do is get a large number of people and make it easy for them to contribute."

Stork acknowledges that such projects might seem less sexy in the eyes of fiction authors and movie directors, but, like Hayes and Hendler, he sees them as a more realistic approach to the future of A.I. research. The quest to build humanlike machines will never go away, because machines already serve as a mirror to the humans who design them. It is unreasonable to expect A.I. researchers to ignore the feelings of curiosity and vanity every human experiences when coming across a mirror. Still, if scientists do want to pursue the goal of human-level intelligence in mechanical systems, they will need to do so riding the market forces and social trends that have made fictional computers like HAL seem so quaint in retrospect.

"I think inside every A.I. researcher, you have that desire to build cognition machines," Stork says. "I wouldn't say the dream has evaporated, but I would say people are a lot more realistic about what we want to do."

———

It may seem awkward to end a book on the debate over artificial intelligence with a chapter on science fiction. But as any science-fiction author will tell you, most stories set in the future are examinations of the present in glittery disguise. As noted in Chapter One, the science of artificial intelligence is a science inextricably linked to the future. The same goes for the debate surrounding that science. Just as movies like *2001* and *A.I.* reflect the concerns and ambitions of their respective ages, recent forward-looking nonfiction works such as *The Age of Spiritual Machines,* "One-Half of a Manifesto," and "Why the Future Doesn't Need Us" offer a Rorschach interpretation of the blurry image that is technological evolution. In each case, the authors lay out future scenarios not so much to predict what will happen as to critique or celebrate current trends in software and machine design.

If anything, works such as *The Age of Spiritual Machines* and "Why the Future Doesn't Need Us" take advantage of the fact that, since the making of *2001,* few fictional and even fewer nonfictional works have been ambitious enough to embrace the future as an illustrative rhetorical tool. Now that the year 2001 has come and gone, authors are once again feeling free enough to offer their own time capsules to the future.

The boundary between nonfiction and science fiction has always been blurry in the A.I. world. In part, this is because the A.I. community has borrowed many of its central terms and ideas from the science-fiction world. It also arises from the community's penchant for treading the fine line between science and hype. Mostly, however, the blurriness grows out of the simple fact that many of the forces that drive and shape A.I. research lurk below the level of conscious thought, in places where fiction writers (and filmmakers) find their best stories and symbolism. Twenty-four centuries after Plato admonished his students to "know thyself" before embarking on any study of the universe, the battle for human self-knowledge and self-awareness still rages. No wonder the notion of machine self-awareness seems a hopeless mirage to some.

That's not to say that today's nonfiction authors shouldn't be held accountable for their predictions. The fact that Kubrick and Clarke's vision of the future remains such an important yardstick for modern A.I. researchers, Stork says, is a testament to the co-authors' prodigious efforts to "get the science right." Whether or not today's authors have matched those efforts remains to be seen. Still, Stork hopes that his book will serve as a precedent when current literary time capsules come due. "So much writing on A.I. is in the 'this will happen in the future' category," Stork says. "These predictions have been shown to be wrong again and again. My book is an attempt to look back at one particular set of predictions and offer a scorecard. What did the authors get right? What did they fail to anticipate? My hope is that today's books will be held to the same standard."

Notes

INTRODUCTION

1. Throughout this book I will be making occasional references to Moore's Law. The term stems from Intel cofounder Gordon Moore's 1965 observation that as integrated-circuit designs improved, the number of transistors per square inch on a top-of-the-line integrated circuit doubled every year. Moore predicted that the trend would continue for at least another decade; when it did, high-tech executives whimsically dubbed the successful prediction "Moore's Law." Nearly four decades later, the trend shows no sign of abating. The rate of doubling seems to have slowed to a period of eighteen to twenty-four months instead of twelve, but continuous advances in microchip design have kept transistor-density growth rates in line with Moore's 1965 prediction. Because transistor density is directly proportional to processor speed and performance, journalists have taken to using Moore's Law as a shorthand term for the overall acceleration of computer performance and, at times, the high-speed evolution of technology itself.
2. Kurzweil, *The Age of Spiritual Machines,* p. 35.
3. Dennett, *Darwin's Dangerous Idea,* p. 521.
4. Ibid., p. 20.

CHAPTER 1. THE INSPIRATION: HILBERT AND TURING

1. Reid, *Hilbert,* p. 17.
2. Turing's paper was published in a 1936–37 volume of *Proceedings of the London Mathematical Society.* A later version, with corrections, ap-

peared in 1937. Church's paper was published in 1936. Source: www. abelard.org.

3. Minsky, *Robotics,* p. 56; Crevier, *AI,* p. 13.

4. Howard Rheingold has written an excellent on-line biography of John von Neumann, summarizing his herculean legacy in the field of computer science and mathematics: www.rheingold.com/texts/tft/4.html.

5. For an extensive on-line biography of Turing, visit: www.turing.org.uk/ turing/bio/part1.html.

CHAPTER 2. THE PIONEER: JOHN MCCARTHY

1. Hilts, *Scientific Temperaments,* p. 218. This 1982 book offers an extensive profile of McCarthy titled "Doll Inside a Doll: John McCarthy and the Evolution of Artificial Intelligence." Hilts documents McCarthy's Marxist upbringing, political views, and current role as the man who, "more or less by himself, upholds the philosophical wing of the study of artificial intelligence." Although a little light on the technical details, it's definitely a good read.

2. Marvin Minsky describes his own early scientific years in Jeremy Bernstein's *Science Observed: Essays Out of My Mind.* Pamela McCorduck's *Machines Who Think* offers an interesting, albeit offbeat, examination of the history of A.I., incuding an extensive look at Minsky's background.

3. Author interview, January 2001.

4. Crevier, *AI,* p. 49.

5. Simon, *Models of My Life,* p. 190.

6. McCorduck, *Machines Who Think,* p. 107.

7. Crevier, *AI,* p. 61.

8. Ibid., pp. 76–77, 148–50.

9. Herbert Simon and Allen Newell, "Heuristic Problem-Solving, the Next Advance in Operations Research," *Journal of the Operations Research Society of America* (1958), vol. 6, no. 1, p. 6. Quoted in Dreyfus, *What Computers Can't Do,* p. xix.

10. Hofstadter, *Gödel, Escher, Bach,* Introduction to 20th Anniversary Edition, p. P-3.

11. Ian Anderson, "A.I. Is Stark Naked from the Ankles Up," *New Scientist* (1984), vol. 104, no. 1430, p. 18.

12. Penrose, *The Emperor's New Mind,* p. 444.

13. Minsky, *Robotics,* p. 24.

CHAPTER 3. THE OPTIMIST: RAY KURZWEIL

1. www.businessweek.com/bwdaily/dnflash/may2001/nf2001052_325.htm.
2. Kurzweil, *The Age of Spiritual Machines,* p. 253.
3. If you'd like to schedule your own ELIZA help session, visit: www -ai.ijs.si/eliza/eliza.html.
4. On page 8 of *The Age of Intelligent Machines,* Kurzweil notes that "the power of computer technology doubles (for the same unit cost) every 18–24 months." In the book's notes, Kurzweil attributes this observation to a survey of power and cost trends published in Tom Forester's book *High-Tech Society.*
5. www.sacredarch.com/thenautilusshellspiral.htm.
6. To read more about networked supercomputer systems, visit: www .beowulf.org.
7. Kurzweil's précis to *The Singularity Is Near* is located at: www .kurzweilai.net/articles/art0134.html?printable=.
8. Vinge's essay "What Is the Singularity?" is located on a number of websites, including: www.ugcs.caltech.edu/~phoenix/vinge/vinge -sing.html.

CHAPTER 4. THE HUMANIST: JARON LANIER

1. E-mail to author.
2. For more on Dawkins, visit: www.world-of-dawkins.com.
3. See Michael C. Perkins, "Jaron Lanier Gets Real," *Red Herring,* June 1, 1993. Also: www.herring.com/index.asp?layout=story&channel= 70000007&doc_id=230015623.
4. For more on Stephen Jay Gould, visit: www.freethought-web.org/ ctrl/news/stephen_gould_additional.html.

CHAPTER 5. THE PESSIMIST: BILL JOY

1. For more on Bill Joy's work with UNIX, read Marshall Kirk McKusick's "20 Years of Berkeley Unix" at: www.oreillynet.com/pub/a/network/ 2000/03/17/bsd.html?page=.
2. http://technetcast/ddj.com/tnc_play_stream.htm/stream_id=186.
3. For more information on nanotechnology development, visit: www

.siliconstrategies.com/story/OEG20001010S0055 and www.yale.edu/ opa/newsr/97-10-10-03.all.html.

4. For more information on nanotechnology, visit the Foresight Institute Web page at: www.foresight.org.

CHAPTER 6. FACT VERSUS FICTION

1. Vincent Lobrutto, *Stanley Kubrick: A Biography* (Cambridge, Mass.: DaCapo Press, 1999), p. 258.

2. Powers, *Galatea 2.2*, p. 199.

Bibliography

Bailey, James. *Afterthought: The Computer Challenge to Human Intelligence.* New York: Basic Books, 1996.

Bernstein, Jeremy. *Science Observed: Essays Out of My Mind.* New York: Basic Books, 1982.

Bulloff, Jack J., Thomas C. Holyoke, and S. W. Hahn, eds. *Foundations of Mathematics: Symposium Papers Commemorating the Sixtieth Birthday of Kurt Gödel.* New York: Springer–Verlag, 1969.

Clarke, Arthur C. *Greetings, Carbon-Based Bipeds! Collected Essays, 1934–1998.* New York: St. Martin's Press, 1999.

Code, Murray. *Myths of Reason: Vagueness, Rationality and the Lure of Logic.* Humanities Press, 1995.

Crevier, Daniel. *AI: The Tumultuous History of the Search for Artificial Intelligence.* New York: Basic Books, 1993.

Davis, Erik. *Techgnosis: Myth, Magic and Mysticism in the Age of Information.* New York: Three Rivers Press, 1998.

Davis, Martin. *The Universal Computer: The Road from Leibniz to Turing.* New York: W. W. Norton & Company, 2000.

Dennett, Daniel C. *Consciousness Explained.* Boston: Little, Brown and Company, 1991.

———. *Darwin's Dangerous Idea: Evolution and the Meanings of Life.* New York: Touchstone, 1996.

Dreyfus, Hubert. *What Computers Can't Do: A Critique of Artificial Reason.* New York: Harper & Row, 1972.

Fang, J. *Towards a Philosophy of Modern Mathematics.* Hauppauge, N.Y.: Paideia Press, 1970.

Fink, Donald G. *Computers and the Human Mind.* Garden City, N.Y.: Anchor Books, 1966.

Gleick, James. *Faster: The Acceleration of Just About Everything.* New York: Vintage Books, 1999.

Havel, David. *Computers Ltd.: What They Really Can't Do.* New York: Oxford University Press, 2000.

Hellman, Hal. *Great Feuds in Science: Ten of the Liveliest Disputes Ever.* New York: John Wiley and Sons, 1998.

Hilts, Philip J. *Scientific Temperaments.* New York: Simon & Schuster, 1982.

Hofstadter, Douglas R. *Gödel, Escher, Bach: An Eternal Golden Braid.* Twentieth-anniversary edition. New York: Basic Books, 1999.

Kurzweil, Ray. *The Age of Intelligent Machines.* Cambridge, Mass.: MIT Press, 1990.

———. *The Age of Spiritual Machines.* New York: Viking, 1999.

Levy, Steven. *Artificial Life: A Report from the Frontier Where Computers Meet Biology.* New York: Vintage Books, 1993.

McCorduck, Pamela. *Machines Who Think: A Personal Inquiry into the History and Prospects of Artificial Intelligence.* San Francisco: W. H. Freeman, 1979.

Minsky, Marvin. *Society of Mind.* New York: Simon & Schuster, 1985.

———, ed. *Robotics.* New York: Doubleday, 1986.

Minsky, Marvin, and Seymour Papert. *Artificial Intelligence.* Condon Lectures. Eugene: Oregon State System of Higher Education, 1973.

Moravec, Hans. *Mind Children.* Cambridge, Mass.: Harvard University Press, 1988.

Newquist, Harvey P. *The Brain Makers: Genius, Ego and Greed in the Quest for Machines That Think.* Indianapolis: Sams Publishing, 1994.

Pais, Abraham. *Subtle Is the Lord . . . : The Science and Life of Albert Einstein.* New York: Oxford University Press, 1982.

Penrose, Roger. *The Emperor's New Mind: Concerning Computers, Minds, and the Laws of Physics.* Oxford: Oxford University Press, 1989.

Pinker, Steven. *How the Mind Works.* New York: W. W. Norton & Company, 1997.

Polya, George. *How to Solve It: A New Aspect of Mathematical Method.* Princeton, N.J.: Princeton University Press, 1945.

Powers, Richard. *Galatea 2.2.* New York: Farrar, Straus & Giroux, 1995.

Reid, Constance. *Hilbert.* New York: Springer–Verlag, 1996.

Roszak, Theodore. *The Cult of Information: A Neo-Luddite Treatise on High*

Tech, Artificial Intelligence and the True Art of Thinking. 2nd ed. Berkeley: University of California Press, 1994.

Simon, Herbert A. Models of My Life. New York: Basic Books, 1992.

Sterelny, Kim. The Representational Theory of Mind: An Introduction. Cambridge, Mass.: Basil Blackwell, 1990.

Stork, David G., ed. HAL's Legacy: 2001's Computer as Dream and Reality. Cambridge, Mass.: MIT Press, 1997.

Teller, Astro. Exegesis. New York: Vintage Books, 1997.

Tiles, Mary. Mathematics and the Image of Reason. New York: Routledge, 1991.

Turkle, Sherry. The Second Self. New York: Simon & Schuster, 1984.

Weizenbaum, Joseph. Computer Power and Human Reason: From Judgment to Calculation. New York: W. H. Freeman and Company, 1976.

Yam, Philip, ed. Scientific American Presents: Exploring Intelligence. New York: Scientific American, Inc., 1998.

Website Resources Directory

Adam's Robot Page: The History of Robotics
http://cache.ucr.edu/~currie/roboadam.htm
Alan Turing: A Short Biography (Part 3—The Turing Machine)
www.turing.org.uk/turing/bio/part3.html
Anselm on God's Existence
www.fordham.edu/halsall/source/anselm.html
Aristotle—biographical overview
www.utm.edu/research/iep/a/aristotl.htm
Artificial Intelligence: History, Philosophy and Practice
http://spinoza.tau.ac.il/hci/dep/philos/ai/links.html
Artificial Intelligence and Connectionism: Some Philosophical
    Implications
www.cts.cuni.cz/~havel/work/ai-cvut.html
Astro Teller
www-2.cs.cmu.edu/~astro/
Autobiography of Herbert A. Simon
www.nobel.se/economics/laureates/1978/simon-autobio.html
Axiomatics
www.ec3.com/990906.htm
Basic Questions Artificial Intelligence FAQ
www-formal.stanford.edu/jmc/whatisai/node1.html#
    SECTION00010000000000000000
The Beowulf Project
www.beowulf.org
Big Blue Wins
www.pbs.org/newshour/bb/entertainment/jan-june97/big_blue_
    5-12.html

Björn's Guide to Philosophy—Kant
www.knuten.liu.se/~bjoch509/philosophers/kan.html
The Blind Watchmaker
www.world-of-dawkins.com/blind.htm
Cellular Automata
http://cgi.student.nada.kth.se/cgi-bin/d95-aeh/get/lifeeng
The Church-Turing Thesis
http://plato.stanford.edu/entries/church-turing/
Computing Machinery and Intelligence
www.abelard.org/turpap/turpap.htm
David Hilbert biography
www-groups.dcs.st-and.ac.uk/~history/Mathematicians/
Hilbert.html
Decidability Questions
www.math.utu.fi/research/automata/decidres.html
Deep Blue Wins
www.research.ibm.com/deepblue/home/html/b.html
Developments in Artificial Intelligence
www.nap.edu/readingroom/books/far/ch9.html#FOOT6
Edge
www.edge.org
ELIZA: A Computer Program for the Study of Natural Language
Communication Between Man and Machine
http://acf5.nyu.edu/~mm64/x52.9265/january1966.html
ENIAC: The Army-Sponsored Revolution
http://ftp.arl.army.mil/~mike/comphist/96summary/
Enigma and Ultra and Information Warfare in World War Two
www.fortunecity.co.uk/underworld/kick/495/enigma.htm
Expert Systems and Artificial Intelligence
http://frederick.itri.loyola.edu/kb/c1_s1.htm
Famous Figures in AI: John McCarthy
www.cs.jcu.edu.au/ftp/web/teaching/Subjects/cp3210/1998/
Assignments/StudentEssays.html#McCarthy-Colby
George Polya: How to Solve It
www.cis.usouthal.edu/misc/polya.html
Gödel's Theorem: An HTML Presentation by Siegfried
www.ddc.net/ygg/etext/godel/
HAL's Birthday Online
www.zdnet.com/yil/content/mag/9703/hal1.html

HAL's Legacy
http://mitpress.mit.edu/e-books/Hal/contents.html
Hans Moravec's home page
www.frc.ri.cmu.edu/~hpm/
Herbert A. Simon: Thinking Machines
www.omnimag.com/archives/interviews/simon.html
Hilbert, David, biographical article
www.britannica.com/eb/article?eu=41309
Hilbert's 23 Unsolved Problems
www.andrews.cdu/~calkins/math/biograph/199899/tophilpr.htm
The History of Artificial Intelligence
http://library.thinkquest.org/2705/history.html
History of Computing: Alan Turing
www.eingang.org/Lecture/turing.html
Hume's "Enquiry Concerning Human Understanding"
www.utm.edu/research/hume/wri/lenq/lenq.htm
IBM Reports Progress in Nanotechnology-Based to Computing
   Devices
www.siliconstrategies.com/story/OEG20001010S0055
Immanuel Kant's "Critique of Pure Reason"
www.arts.cuhk.edu.hk/Philosophy/Kant/cpr/
The Implications of Gödel's Theorem
http://users.ox.ac.uk/~jrlucas/implgoed.html
It's Only Checkers, but the Computer Taught Itself
www.cs.buffalo.edu/~rapaport/572/S01/checkers.html
It's 2001. Where Is HAL?
http://technetcast.ddj.com/tnc_play_stream.html?
   stream_id=526
Jaron
www.wired.com/wired/archive//1.02/jaron.html
Jaron Lanier Gets Real
www.herring.com/index.asp?layout=story&channel=
   70000007&doc_id=230015623
John McCarthy
http://henson.cc.kzoo.edu/~k98ww01/mccarthy.html
John McCarthy: Artificial Intelligence
www.omnimag.com/archives/interviews/mccarthy.html
John McCarthy's home page
http://www-formal.Stanford.EDU/jmc/

A Killer App for Computer Chat
www.economist.com/displayStory.cfm?Story_ID=197730
Kurt Gödel's Ontological Argument
www.stats.uwaterloo.ca/~cgsmall/ontology.html
The Last Generalist: An Interview with Richard Powers
http://eserver.org/clogic/2-2/williams.html
The Law of Accelerating Returns
www.kurzweilai.net/articles/art0134.html?printable=
Logical vs. Analogical or Symbolic vs. Connectionist or Neat vs.
Scruffy
www.ai.mit.edu/people/minsky/papers/SymbolicVs.
Connectionist.txt
Ludwig Wittgenstein (1889–1951)
www.utm.edu/research/iep/w/wittgens.htm
Marvin Minsky and a Common Sense Knowledge Base
http://csel.cs.colorado.edu/~cs3202/papers/
Muneeb_Cheema.html
Mellow Techno Rock in the Park
www.wired.com/news/culture/0,1284,38032,00.html
Minds, Brains and Programs
http://members.aol.com/NeoNoetics/MindsBrains
Programs.html
Minds, Machines and Gödel
http://users.ox.ac.uk/~jrlucas/mmg.html
Moore's Law
http://webopedia.internet.com/TERM/M/Moores_Law.html
National Tele-Immersion Initiative
www.advanced.org/teleimmersion.html
The Nautilus Shell Spiral
www.sacredarch.com/thenautilusshellspiral.htm
Nerd of the Week: Ray Kurzweil
www.nerdworld.com/lf_notw_014.html
Non-Euclidean Geometries
www.cut-the-knot.com/triangle/pythpar/NonEuclid.html
On Computable Numbers, with an Application to the
Entscheidungsproblem
www.abelard.org/turpap2/turpap2.htm
One-Half of a Manifesto
www.wired.com/wired/archive/8.12/lanier.html

One Too Many? The Role of Euclid's Fifth Postulate in the
    Development of Non-Euclidean Geometries
    www.zarquonmedia.com/writing/sci/role_of_euclids_fifth_
    postulate_on_non-euclidean_geometry.html
Open Mind Initiative
    www.OpenMind.org/index.shtml
The Open Source Definition
    www.opensource.org/docs/definition.html
Programs with Common Sense
    www-formal.stanford.edu/jmc/mcc59/mcc59.html
A Proposal for the Dartmouth Summer Research Project on Artificial
    Intelligence
    www-formal.stanford.edu/jmc/history/dartmouth/dartmouth.html
Pygmalion and Galatea in Myth
    www.loggia.com/myth/galatea.html
Rants and Raves: "Why the Future Doesn't Need Us"
    www.wired.com/wired/archive/8.07/rants_pr.html
Ray Kurzweil: Curriculum Vitae
    www.kurzweiltech.com/raycv.htm
Remembrance of Future Past
    www.sciam.com/0197issue/0197review2.html
René Descartes and the Legacy of Mind/Body Dualism
    http://serendip.brynmawr.edu/exhibitions/Mind/Descartes.html
R.U.R.
    http://pimacc.pima.edu/~gmcmillan/rur.html
Q&A with Kurzweil's Ray Kurzweil
    www.businessweek.com/1998/08/b3566022.htm
Searle's Chinese Box: Debunking the Chinese Room Argument
    http://members.aol.com/lshauser2/chinabox.html
Scientists, Fans Mark HAL's Birthday
    http://web.mit.edu/newsoffice/tt/1997/jan15/43204.html
StarLink Recall Climbs to 300 Different Items
    www.purefood.org/ge/starlink300.cfm
Stephen Jay Gould
    www.freethought-web.org/ctrl/news/stephen_gould_
    additional.html
Tools for Thought, Chapters Four and Five
    www.rheingold.com/texts/tft/4.html
    www.rheingold.com/texts/tft/5.html

Turing Machine
http://plato.stanford.edu/entries/turing-machine/
What Futures Shall We Make?
www-formal.stanford.edu/jmc/future/index.html
What Is a Turing Machine?
www.alanturing.net/pages/Reference%20Articles/
What%20is%20a%20Turing%20Machine.html
What Is the Singularity?
www.ugcs.caltech.edu/~phoenix/vinge/vinge-sing.html
Why People Think Computers Can't
ftp://ftp.ai.mit.edu/pub/minsky/ComputersCantThink.txt
Why the Future Doesn't Need Us
www.wirednews.com/wired/archive/8.04/joy.html
Will Calhoun
www.willcalhoun.com
Will Robots Inherit the Earth?
www.ai.mit.edu/people/minsky/papers/sciam.inherit.txt
Yale Scientists Measure Current Across Single Organic Molecule,
Paving Way for Development of Radically New Transistors
www.yale.edu/opa/newsr/97-10-10-03.all.html

About the Author

SAM WILLIAMS is a freelance writer whose commentaries on software and software culture have appeared in Upside Today (www.upside.com) and BeOpen.com. He also writes for numerous magazines, newspapers, and, when the spirit moves him, television programs. He currently lives in Brooklyn, New York, with his wife, Tracy.

About AtRandom.com Books

AtRandom.com Books, a new imprint within the Random House Trade Group, is dedicated to publishing original books that harness the power of new technologies. Each title, commissioned expressly for this publishing program, will be offered simultaneously in various digital formats and as a trade paperback.

AtRandom.com books are designed to provide people with choices about their reading experience and the information they can obtain. They are aimed at communities of highly motivated readers who want immediate access to substantive and artful writing on the various subjects that fascinate them.

Our list features expert writing on health, business, technology, culture, entertainment, law, finance, and a variety of other topics. Whether written in a spirit of play, rigorous critique, or practical instruction, these books possess a vitality that new ways of publishing can aptly serve.

For information about AtRandom.com Books and to sign up for our e-newsletters, visit www.atrandom.com.